guerrilla
theater

guerrilla theater

SCENARIOS FOR REVOLUTION

BY JOHN WEISMAN

ANCHOR BOOKS

ANCHOR PRESS/DOUBLEDAY

GARDEN CITY, NEW YORK

1973

The Anchor Books edition is the first publication of *Guerrilla Theater*.

Thanks to the people at the theaters. And to Coolie, Bob Levinson, Ronnie Shushan, Digby Diehl, Al Kamuda, and, of course, Nancy.

Anchor Books edition: 1973

ISBN: 0-385-08065-4
Library of Congress Card Catalog Number 72–89679
Copyright © 1973 by John Weisman
All Rights Reserved
Printed in the United States of America

Acknowledgments
Cover photo by the author.

Luis Valdez and El Teatro Campesino, for permission to use photographs; "Notes on Chicano Theater"; and the plays, *La Quinta Temporada* and *Los Vendidos:* Copyright © 1972 by Luis Valdez for El Teatro Campesino. All rights reserved. The actos are the sole property of El Teatro Campesino, and are fully protected by copyright. All dramatic, motion picture, radio and television rights are strictly reserved. No performance, professional or amateur, or any broadcast, or any public reading or recitation may be given without written permission in advance. All inquiries should be addressed to Luis Valdez, P. O. Box 274, San Juan Bautista, California 95045. (408) 623-4436.

Ed Bereal and the Bodacious Buggerrilla, for permission to use excerpts from interviews; photographs; and the plays *Uncle Tom, 1984,* and *Killer Joe,* Copyright © 1972 by Bodacious Buggerrilla.

San Francisco Mime Troupe, for permission to use photographs; and for the play *Telephone,* Copyright © 1969 by San Francisco Mime Troupe, Inc. Performance rights reserved. Contact: San Francisco Mime Troupe, 450 Alabama Street, San Francisco, California 94110.

Street Player's Union, for permission to use *Smile.*

City Street Theater, for permission to use *Three Improvisations.*

Leonard Smith and Concept East Theater, for permission to use excerpts from interviews; photographs; and the play *White Sale* by Demani Abakar, Copyright © 1972 by Concept East Theater. All rights reserved. Contact Leonard Smith, Concept East Theater, 60 East Harper, Detroit, Michigan.

For Daniel and Luis Valdez;
In Memory of George and Jonathan Jackson

CONTENTS

LIST OF PLAYS

THE OBSERVER

Our American theater has always been white-oriented and escapist in nature. Even in the thirties—those times of social ferment often thrown in our faces by today's theatrical liberals ("Remember Odets, Elmer Rice, and Robert Anderson . . . now there, my boy, were *real* revolutionaries. None of your two-bit punks like Ed Bullins.")—the theater was chiefly a means of emotional escape. There was indeed political action and some didacticism that called for change, but the call kept itself well within the already defined boundaries of American society. Nowhere were there street riots such as Berlin had experienced as a result of the premiere of Erwin Piscator's *Red Rumble*. But then, Germans had the *Freikorps* and machine-gun politics, while on the home front we were content with KKK lynchings, Al Capone, and J. Edgar Hoover. Even the Communist Party, America's bunch of pre-McCarthy revolutionaries, dogmatized that societal change could take place within the existing political framework. Remember, if you will, all those Communist candidates.

Most of the "good" (read "accepted") theater of our generation has continued to typify the bent of middle-class American society. Most often, it is imitative art, reflecting upon where we stand now rather than pointing out new directions for us to go. Its innovations tend these days toward nudity and four-letter words, making theater at its best entertaining and enlightening, and at its worst, resembling canned soup in maudlin tastelessness, lack of integrity, and vigor.

White actors, technicians, and directors who drop out of the middle-class, button-down shuck soon find they have no place to go, either on or off Broadway. Regional theaters, engaged in their never-ending rat race for foundation grants and government support, are also a dead end. Cultural centers in many cities provide a panacea, but it is a panacea for the moneyed classes—those cultured elite to whom the plays are aimed. The "others" watch the tube, often gaining a glimpse of the elite crowd at a Civic Center opening on the late news.

Blacks and Latinos, too, have no place in the establishment's theater. Despite the House Nigger (called NUF, or Nigger Up Front, at most resident theater companies) and an occasional brown face in the crowd, they are for the most part eschewed by what has rightly been identified as a cynical, hypocritical, white liberal power structure that talks a good game but passes when the chips are down.

The result of this cultural segregation has been the growth of a new minority theater in America. Along with the often violent political upheaval that is taking place (no matter how much it's denied in the conservative press, there were in 1970 more than five thousand separate acts of insurrection done in this country), disenfranchised whites, reds, blacks, and *bronces* have discovered that theater is a tool that not only entertains, but that can also be used to raise their cultures' consciousness. They see that it can reflect, interpret, convey, record, and sometimes even lead a revolution.

What has evolved over the past decade is a theater that seeks to force change in America by preaching a whole new set of values and priorities to its audiences, values that often have nothing whatsoever to do with any previously established social order or system. It can be called guerrilla, radical, alternative, street, or people's theater. In a sense it is all of these: guerrilla because it exists to do running battles with the establishment, then retreat into the invisibility of the community (Watts, Harlem, Berkeley, the *barrio*). Radical it is in the true sense of the word—basic. Guerrilla theater is basic theater. No frills, no Gower Champion dances. No Edward Albee bitchiness. It's theater from the gut instead of the intellect. Radical theater is alternative theater because it provides perhaps the only artistic alternative to the cultural mess we're into today. It is (to use an establishment definition) the radical's answer to his identity crisis, if he's theatrically oriented.

And alternative theater is street theater because, much of the time, no self-respecting middle-class highbrow theater would let a scroungy bunch of artistic revolutionaries in its doors. (Note: Middle-class theater folk are often scroungy, too. But look closely and you'll see they've been effectively deodorized.) It's also street theater because the street is where you find people. And street theater is people's theater, partly because it exists for everyone who's willing to stand around and watch it, but mainly because it *belongs* to the people—its audience—instead of to the foundations, the government, or to any board of directors.

Guerrilla theater is hard to analyze. Since it exists for a specific audience, and since most critics are from the white establishment, they deal with it as they would deal with either *Hair* or *Oh! Calcutta!* depending on whether they have Broadway or off-Broadway proclivities. For that reason, most guerrilla theaters don't care for critics. In any event, critics are irrelevant to such theaters since the theaters' success is measured by either a new sociopolitical awareness on the part of their audience, by the money in the hat that's passed around after a performance, or both. Fifty cents and 150 shouts of "Go home, you dirty motherfuckers" from an audience of 150 people means either the theater's bad or it's in the wrong neighborhood.

Guerrilla theater is neighborhood theater. It's at its most effective when performed inside the community for which it was created. Ed Bereal of Los Angeles' Bodacious Buggerrilla says that when his company performs outside of Watts, the performance is cut by often more than half an hour, "because although the cats outside may dig us, we're not gettin' the same responses we get when we're talkin' to our own folks."

Some "neighborhoods" extend farther than others. Luis Valdez—who began El Teatro Campesino in 1965 as a theatrical adjunct to Cesar Chavez's United Farmworker's Union—has toured throughout the country, spawning more than fifteen new *teatros* in the Southwest alone.

Guerrilla theater is exciting theater. The basic problem with establishment theaters, whether they're on or off Broadway, regional, repertory, or stock houses, is ennui. Producers cry about lack of audience support, and regional artistic directors say again and again that the only way they can survive and do "serious" drama is through foundation support and government grants. In one of his more coherent statements, André Gregory, one of Regional Theater's Grand Old Men, once said that before the resident companies in this country have matured, they'll have "bored the shit out of millions of people." The repertoire of the establishment proves it repeatedly. Time and again the same warhorses are dragged out for another go-round: *The Cherry Orchard, Uncle Vanya, Death of a Salesman,* and *Charley's Aunt* clog the stages of resident theaters with somnolent regularity. By broadening their artistic outlook and making guerrilla theater *people's* theater, the radicals are creating new and hitherto untapped audiences. By simplifying the act of theater, by making it not only entertaining but accessible, understandable, and exciting, guerrilla troupes make the audience want to see more.

Even more important, however, are guerrilla theater's political and social goals. The radical artistic directors, playwrights, and companies tend to view theater as a social instrument. It doesn't just entertain; it motivates, arouses, and organizes. It is didactic without being preachy, educational without resorting to pedanticism. The way it achieves these things is through the use of something almost unknown in the commercial theater: real people.

"If you want unbourgeois theater," says Luis Valdez, pulling at his ever-present cigar, "then you better goddamn well find unbourgeois people to do it." Valdez is a case in point. Born near Delano, and educated ("when I wasn't in the fields, picking") in California's rural public schools, he looks, dresses, and talks like the people for whom his company performs—the California *campesinos* and their *pachuco* counterparts in the cities' *barrios*. The original company of the Teatro was made up of *campesinos* with no theatrical training at all. Now, Valdez uses a mélange of students and workers. Like most guerrilla troupes, he has refused outside grants and financial aid: "If we got, say, ten thousand dollars for the Teatro, then our lifestyle would go up. We'd buy expensive costumes and equipment, and the people would say, 'No dice. You got money now and you're better than we are.' So screw the grants. I'd rather be a part of the community than a visitor to it. The Teatro is built on the assumption that it satisfies a need of the people. If we go beyond them or above them, then we're just jerking off."

In political *raisons d'être*, guerrilla theaters have their chief motivating force. What all of them are saying, whether they come from the black, white, brown, red, or yellow communities, is that there is something rotten about our present Western, capitalist American society. Unlike "socially oriented" theater groups like The Committee, The Second City, or The Firesign Theater, most guerrilla troupes exist not only to identify the problems, but to provide some solutions. The kinds of revolution that they talk about vary, from violent overthrow of the existing system to peaceful revolution through cultural awareness. They often become chameleonlike, changing the intensity of the pitch with every audience. Each is committed to agitprop (read "agitation and propaganda") aesthetics as an effective way of talking to their brothers.

Three years ago there were no more than fifty guerrilla companies in America. Now there are closer to ten times that number. As the revolutionary movement in this country grows stronger, the need for and impact of radical people's theaters in ghettos, *barrios,* prisons, even in schools, will grow stronger along with it.

It is senseless, as well as unnecessary, to proceed with a heavy analysis of guerrilla theaters. They are, by design, in a constant state of flux. Their movement is what keeps them close to the people and the revolution. Hence to discuss them in mere analysis would be to do them a disservice; they don't exist to be studied—they exist to be seen and heard.

It is what the practitioners of radical theater have to say about the subject that becomes, finally, the analysis of guerrilla theater, just as it is by the audience's actions after the play that revolutionary theater justifies its own existence.

JOHN WEISMAN
Los Angeles, 1971
Detroit, 1972

THE PARTICIPANT

AS SEEN BY THE AUTHOR

Fade in on the Cal State Community Center in South Los Angeles. A narrow hall has been transformed into a theater through the addition of an 18-inch platform at one end and 150 chairs with an aisle running down the middle of the room. Walls painted glossy black. Posters of Angela, Malcolm X, Eldridge, Bobby. Cast as audience young blacks, easily mistaken for just plain folks from the neighborhood: students, community workers, etc. Noise from outside room where Panther literature, prison newspapers, etc., are for sale. AUDIENCE *should be talking about what's happening in the neighborhood, relatives and friends recently busted, etc.*

The READER should at this point answer out loud as to how many of his relatives and close friends are currently serving time.

For sound effects, jazz or R&B. Play it loud. Keep the lighting simple. Three or four photofloods will do.
Enter UNCLE SAM, *dressed in white toga, top hat of red, white, and blue. Whiteface. His cape is an Amerikan flag. General laughter.*
UNCLE SAM *smiles.*

"Niggers. . . .

"Niggers, you foul, smelly mothafuckers. . . .

"NIGGERS, I'M TALKING TO YOU!"

(*A* BYSTANDER *peers into the theater and sees the raving* SAM *onstage.* BYSTANDER *looks at his* FRIEND, *still talking around the corner.*)

"Hey, Jim, these dudes got some heavy fuckin' shit goin' on. Stick your head in here and dig on this. . . ."

(*Cross fade to Soledad Prison. Interior shot of library. One hundred fifty Chicano* INMATES *with only one* PIG *to guard them. No stage necessary.*

(*Curtain hung between two poles with sign that reads:* El Teatro Campesino.

(INMATES *talking softly about the most recent stabbings and guard abuses.*

(*Enter* DANNY VALDEZ *with a guitar.*)

"We're here to tell you about what's happening in the Bronce world outside. It's a dose of real life—no bullshit about how great it is to be a Mexican here in occupied Aztlan.

"The first acto is about the kind of people that put you all here in the first place—the sellouts that make their living from our Mexican blood. It's called *Los Vendidos. Viva La Causa!*" (*A* PRISONER *looks directly into the camera. He's been in Soledad for six years.*)

"This is the first decent thing that I've seen since I've been here. You know, man, I'm amazed that the pigs let you all in—Valdez is into some heavy shit.

"Don't worry, though—even though we got only one pig in the room, there are six more outside (*he gestures at the row of open windows that face the prison infirmary*) on that shotgun rail you can see. Ain't it a bitch?"

(*Cross fade to a street in Berkeley. A political rally for the April coalition, soon to take three seats on the Berkeley City Council. Cast this scene with a mélange of street people, acid freaks, professional liberals, students, and disinterested onlookers. Use lots of dogs and children.*

(*Dolly in on four long-haired* FREAKS *who unpack a snare drum, bass, tuba, cornet, and guitar from a number of broken-down suitcases.*

(*The* CROWD *sits down, blocking the street. The* FREAKS *begin an impromptu concert. The music should have overtones of Brecht and Weil. The whole scene should be reminiscent of a George Grosz cartoon redrawn by R. Crumb.*

(*The song stops. One of the* FREAKS *begins to speak.*)

"We're the East Bay Sharks. Your theater. Berkeley's own civic theater. We're going to do a juicy little tale for you called *Thimblewoman* or, *Alice and the Amazing Magic Cockroach*, and when we're done, you can help us out. When the hat's passed around, feed a hungry Shark. Feed the Sharks by putting some bread in the hat."

(*Cross fade to the interior of Concept East's Theater in Detroit. Volunteer laborers are busy painting the gym—formerly the Sale-*

*sian High School—black. The old school has recently been acquired
by Concept as its new Black Theater and Cultural Center.*

(*Pan up to a fifteen-foot scaffolding. On top of it,* LEONARD SMITH,
*Concept's executive director. He is twenty-eight, tall, with a Fu
Manchu mustache. On his head is a paper bag, protecting his Afro
from splattering paint.*

(SMITH *puts his roller down, sits on the edge of his high platform,
and looks at the camera.*)

"When LeRoi started writing, the whole black theater thing was
'kill whitey, kill whitey, kill whitey!' Now we've gone farther than
that. It's time to get the brothers together—make them aware that
their black roots tie them together.

"Shit, man, black theater's got to say something about where we
all are. It's got to face up to life—from the brother in the slam to
the pimp jivin' with a string of broads. Y'know, black theater don't
have *time* to get into that 'kill whitey, kill whitey, kill whitey!' trip
any more. I mean, man, like who the fuck has time to give a goddamn about whitey any more?

"See what I mean?"

(*Slow fade to black. Fade in on* THE WRITER. *A bare office. Typing
sounds. Voice over this section.*)

Cultural revolutionaries? The words are pretentious and pre-
sumptuous. Not guerrillas, either, at least not in the way we've
come to know the word.

Who are they and who am I? What's my stake in all this, anyhow? The book I guess, but there's more.

Where does it come from—where did it start for me?

Genesis of motive.

I remember in 1964, I got out into the neighborhoods of New
York with Joseph Papp's New York Shakespeare Festival. We did
fifty-nine performances of *A Midsummer Night's Dream* in thirty-
nine parks. It was the first time I could actually remember meeting
an audience face to face. They confronted us, and we had to talk
to them—before, during, and after the show. Theatrical revolution, right? Answer: No. But it was a start. It was some kind of a
beginning.

It was a start because I discovered that audiences were made up
of real people, who wanted to be entertained; and at the same time,
I discovered that we weren't doing much to make each neighborhood's audience into a whole.

The Mobile Theater could entertain, but it couldn't change, because it was just passing through. And making things change is what this is all about. All right. Force change.

Where?

In the community. Do it from within.

How?

As best you know how. Theater people do theater. But do it so that it answers the needs of the people you've got as an audience, not to satisfy your own fucking ego. But the key is: STAY IN THE NEIGHBORHOOD.

Why stay in the neighborhood?

Well, because of the way this country is set up. Artists are unique, creative people. All they have to sell is themselves. If they're bought, by museums, by civic groups, by the government—by any of the buyers in Amerika—they rise above their communities economically. They sell to the rich, because the poor can't afford art.

APHORISM: THERE ARE NO POOR FOLKS' ARTISTS IN AMERIKA TODAY; JUST ARTISTS WHO ARE POOR, FOLKS.

So: Stay in the neighborhood so you can talk with the people on the block, whatever size the block is, and do theater that satisfies their needs.

This book is a collection of scenarios for revolution—all kinds of scenarios, for all kinds of revolutions. Treat it like a play. Watch it and talk with it. Listen, participate.

Do it.

Begin, say, with a theater game: a world game; an improvisation.

EL MUNDO: *Creación Colectiva* (written after Luis Valdez).

Semispontaneous characterizations within a situation, ending with a solution to the dramatic problem,

Playing time: As long as it takes to read this.

Actors and participants may take weeks, months, or years to plan characters, conflicts, crises, conclusions, etc.

Begin with: "We are all outlaws in the eyes of Amerika. . . ."

west coast
letters

Travelodge Motel
Fresno, California

Dear Nancy

It's a long, hot drive from Los Angeles across the Tehachapi
Mountains into the San Joaquin Valley, the spine of California's
agricultural plain. Coming down the north side of the pass, the
mountains divide, leaving in the front of the windshield a broad,
exquisitely multicolored expanse of fertile, well-manicured, and
irrigated lands, filled with all the fruit and vegetable goodies that
wind up in such places as Detroit and Sandusky.

A trip here into central California is like a trip back in time. Even
after the considerable success of Cesar Chavez and the Farmworkers' Union, the San Joaquin Valley is still a feudal place, where small
numbers of growers and agricultural combines hold really fantastic
strength. The monied people control everything, from the election
of local judges and school boards to the selection of the district
water commissioners—an important post in the valley, where irri-
gation is everything.

I drove out of Bakersfield on Highway 99, heading almost due
north, parallel with railroad tracks on which freights still carry
free riders. Only today's riders are a mixture of Campesinos, jumping from job to job, and longhairs, riding boxcars between spells
of hitchhiking on their way to Los Angeles or San Francisco. Along
the road, which is freeway-wide, there are stands that sell olives,
dates, grapes, and honey. They're disappearing, though, and will
die out by the time superhighway No. 5 is finished, sometime next
year.

Off the main road, though, it's really something else. It took about
half of the trip to rid me of my city kid's naïveté. The migrant worker's world of *The Grapes of Wrath* still exists in 1971. Shacks made
of cardboard cartons with dirt floors are the homes for thousands
of Chicano, Filipino, and white workers, literally condemned in
impossible-to-quit serfdom to the master-growers. Driving north on
Highway 99 is an education: I felt that things were bad; I just never
knew that they were this bad. Or this real.

You know what's real? Sweat is real. And heat. Oppressive, sear-
ing, hellish heat. Twenty-four hours ago I would have said that what

I saw today—the way people live—is impossible here in California.

Like the fantastic wealth and incredible poverty that exist side by side. On Highway 98, just west of Fresno, I saw a white house by the roadside. The house looked newly painted, and had two brand-new autos in the garage; opposite was a shack surrounded by a broken fence. There were a couple of chickens scratching in the shack's front yard, and a half-naked kid making mudpies by the fence. The white house belongs to a farmer who owns seventy-eight acres of grapes. He's also got some cattle and some chickens. The shack belongs to his full-time hired hand, who pays the farmer fifty dollars a month rent on the place. When I asked for a bathroom, the maid working in the white house took one look at my hair and told me to "try across the street." So, the farmer has central air conditioning; his Chicano hired hand has an outhouse, which I used, and which stank.

Like I said, even without taking into consideration meeting Luis Valdez and seeing the Teatro Campesino, the day's been an education for me.

I'm still awed by the farmworkers. Somehow, I've managed to exist more than a quarter of a century without ever seeing people work in the fields. Today, it was impossible *not* to see them. Old, young, single people, whole families. Filipinos, Bronces, whites, blacks, filling boxes with everything from strawberries to grapes for the raisin plant in Kingsburg. It was like looking at a Goya painting. I flashed on that. I remember when I was a kid in New York looking at Goya's stuff and thinking what a great imagination he had. He wasn't imagining, though, he was painting life.

Stopped in Delano to see if I could talk to Cesar Chavez. He wasn't there, but I had a look at the town where the farmworkers' movement got started. Rural California, circa 1971.

What? Karl's Shoe Store, Beneficial Finance, McDonald's. Lots of crumbly WPA sidewalks. Slums, all sun-baked and hot.

At the north end of town, close by the Surplus City, I listened to two farmers talk. Their necks were as red and creased as turkey croups.

"Fifty goddamn years of fuckin' profit, and those spic sons of bitches are tryin' to take it all away from us now."

"It's the fuckin' kids," says the other. "Ought to fuckin' run 'em outta town back to Fritoland, where they belong."

And that's what Cesar Chavez came into when he started the

farmworkers' union in '62. And also what Luis Valdez found when he got the Teatro together in '65.

History? Chavez started in 1962. But it wasn't until the spring of 1965 that he had enough support to strike, which he did against the Martin Ranch. That victory was almost Pyrrhic. In the fall of '65, Delano erupted into a series of violent confrontations between growers and workers. Strikers were run down by trucks, spat on, and sprayed with poisonous insecticides. The police, of course, just stood by. "The white heat of Delano" is how Luis Valdez describes it.

In 1965, Luis Valdez was twenty-three. He had worked his way through San Jose State, majoring in speech and drama. In his last year of college, he wrote a play called *The Shrunken Head of Pancho Villa,* which dealt with Chicano pride—Luis called it a play about cultural rebirth.

One of the problems that Chavez faced was organizing what amounted to a peasant mass into a political force. And when Luis came from San Francisco, where he had been performing with the San Francisco Mime Troupe, Cesar found an effective way of organizing—through theater.

But that's getting ahead of myself. What you should know now is what I found when I got to Fresno. The Teatro is headquartered in the barrio—the ghetto—on a tree-lined corner. I wandered around the streets for a while. Orange trees in backyards, and lemon trees, too. Old cars. The barrio is east of the center of Fresno, where there's a new mall, some motels, like the one I'm staying at, and even a couple of passable restaurants, I'm told.

The Teatro, though, stays in the ghetto. It's a community organization; it's always been one. When I arrived, there were a group of carpenters building a portable stage in the courtyard. Young Chicanos, with power tools and carpenters' aprons. Made me think of my days at the Shakespeare Festival in New York—where we believed in what we were doing, worked for fifty bucks a week, and were all—carpenters, propmen, grips, electricians—Serious Artists To Be Reckoned With. The cats building the stage had that same look to them.

Finally found Luis in the Teatro office—lots of desks, piles and piles of huelgista literature, masks, costume and prop boxes, and five people trying to talk to him at once. He's a short dude, maybe five-six, stocky build, a great long Pancho Villa mustache that droops around his mouth, and a long cigar chomped in his teeth. Twinkling eyes. I liked him instinctively. Wears work clothes— brown shirt, black, pegged pants, and nondescript black shoes.

The thing that struck me most about Luis was his energy. He radiates vitality, life. And he's convinced that his kind of theater— people's theater—is the way to create a cultural renaissance in the Chicano community. He's a pragmatist, I think, and a believer in theater as a way of life. Got a wife and two children, and a brother, Daniel, who is part of the Teatro.

We spent some time walking around the Teatro's grounds. Looked at the stage—a hexagonal wooden platform that sits on many sawhorse-type legs—which he told me was copied from the San Francisco Mime Troupe's portable one. Then we sat down in a backroom, with a couple of burritos, some Coca-Cola, and my notebook.

In conversation, he's an earnest cat. There was very little bullshit flowing, because he's beyond bullshit. There's a job to do, and, Luis feels, not enough time to do it.

"If you want to do unbourgeois theater," he said, sounding a lot like a Chicano Bertolt Brecht, "you got to find unbourgeois people to do it."

The Teatro was born in Delano, California. Workers, confused, remained loyal to the contractors and growers, because that was the established order, and you got your head smashed if you bucked it. The bosses, sensing their advantage, used the labor camps where the workers lived to combat the union—they'd split up families, forcing men to live in one camp and women in another, or have separate camps for blacks, browns, and whites. Some of that is still happening today. What's also happening is that the contractors are getting their labor from towns like Fresno, and busing them for sometimes two or three hours each way. What happens, then, is that a man will get up at 4 A.M., ride a bus until seven, work until seven in the evening, and then have to ride, dog-tired, back to town. It doesn't make for a lot of rest.

In his student years at San Jose State, Luis had gone home to Delano during the summers to work, but hadn't really gotten into the union struggle. It was only when he got to the San Francisco Mime Troupe, right after finishing school, that he saw a viable way of making theater work for the Chicano workers in the San

Joaquin Valley. And he was with the Mime Troupe when the strike
got into its heavy period.

What was needed more than anything was a way of making the
people see the advantages of the union, the need to form a cohesive, active community, and, underlying these things, a way to make
Chicanos proud to be Bronces.

What he did was suggest to Chavez that a small group of players
equipped with guitars who could infiltrate the camps and buses
might be more effective than an organizer with a handful of political pamphlets. Chavez agreed to try the idea, and Valdez went
out onto the picket lines to recruit players for his guerrilla troupe.

Among those he found were Felipe Cantu, a worker in his forties.
A man with practically no formal education, Cantu was a vocifer-
ous natural performer, engaged in haranguing the scabs who
crossed picket lines to work in the fields. When Valdez first saw
him, he was in the midst of a wild, comic pantomime, acting out
his interpretation of a drunken scab tortured by his conscience.

There was also Augustin Lira, songwriter and grape and melon
picker, whose lyrics were born in the cardboard hovels that farmers
use to house the field hands. And Gilbert Rubio, who at eighteen
had picked cotton in Texas for fifty cents an hour, and grapes in
California for little more. Everyone Valdez recruited had different
backgrounds, with education varying from none to college degrees.
But they had one common bond: the sweaty back and bruised
hands of the field laborer. And they had one common need: to communicate with their fellow workers.

The first time the Teatro met was in the UFW's offices, a small
house that served as union hall and living quarters for Chavez and
his people. Luis talked for a while, explaining that the goals of the
theater were political. He tried to tell his actors how they would
succeed, but no one understood. Finally, in desperation, he took
two hastily lettered signs saying HUELGISTA (striker) and
ESQUIROL (scab), and hung them around the necks of two people. He told the "scab" to act like one. Then, according to Luis, "all
hell broke loose. All of a sudden people started coming into the
house from I don't know where. They started changing signs around
and people started volunteering. "Let me play so and so." They
were everywhere—the doorways, the living room, even outside the
windows looking in! I found out that night you can do a lot by
acting things out."

From these first improvisations, Luis formulated a series of actos, short one-act plays that dealt with the problems of the workers and the importance of organizing into a union. At first he considered doing works by Lope de Vega or Tirso de Molina, which he knew had originally been performed on small stages. But the drawback to doing classics was their not being accepted by the audience. Aesthetic enjoyment had to have meaning for the workers. So instead of arlecchinos, pantalones, or brighellas, Valdez wrote original plays for esquiroles, contratistas (contractors), patroncitos (bosses), and huelgistas.

The acto, according to Luis, is the best form for the Teatro's plays, because they're short, punchy, and funny. The social commentary plays of the thirties, filled with cries for justice, equality, and union organization, were complex productions. The acto form enables the Teatro to be highly mobile. It can travel in two small panel trucks, with everything (including actors) jammed inside.

The acto is loosely put together but highly stylized. Signs hang from the actors, telling the audience who they portray. Gestures are as exaggerated as Chaplin or Buster Keaton; the boss always flicks his cigar as if he had been taught by Groucho Marx. Scripts are loose, skeletons of what happens on stage. But they read well, because they are intensely dramatic, moving, caustic bits of writing, which the entire Teatro helps put together.

One of the first actos, and one of the most popular and effective, is *La Quinta Temporada* (*The Fifth Season*). Luis named the contratista "El Coyote," because contractors fed off the workers, taking kickbacks from them as well as from the Patrón, who pays well for cheap labor.

The play shows that workers without a contract are helpless at the hands of big business. As fast as the worker stuffs his pockets with money, picked feverishly from an actor plastered with cash and labeled "summer" or "fall," it is stolen from him and given back to the Patrón by El Coyote, who skims his share from the top. Just as in real life, a worker's wages are taken by company stores that charge high prices for food and clothing, or exorbitant rent for substandard housing. It is only when the worker holds out, at great personal cost and risk, that the union, the churches, and La Raza—the whole Mexican-American race—are able to win the fight for the Fifth Season—the season of social justice, who boots El Coyote offstage to the cheers of the audience.

Luis said that *The Fifth Season* is successful because it hits home yet is still funny in a highly slapstick way. "When 'Summer' comes on, wearing an old shirt with money all over it . . . with that image we've hit on something. This is the way that farmworkers look at summer. And the image carries through to other audiences, too, although perhaps at a different level." The propaganda is as subtle as a cream pie in the face. But it works—directly transmitting the idea to the audience, and reaping the reward of instantaneous understanding.

During the fall, winter, and spring, the Teatro goes out on tour to colleges and universities all over the southwestern United States. In the summer, they stay close to Fresno, mapping out strategy for the coming season, going on weekends to small towns in the valley to play to Chicanos. Summer is the hardest time for the Teatro, because it performs without charge for the workers, and travel expenses are hard to come by.

Audiences are often small—two or three hundred at a time—but this, Luis feels, is only natural, since the towns themselves are small, and threat of economic reprisal by the monied classes is great. As Cesar Chavez said, workers were afraid to come out in favor of the union, even by the act of coming to see the Teatro. Even so, Chavez used the Teatro when regular organizers met with failure. In one small town near Selma, California, the Teatro succeeded in convincing field hands of the need to organize after UFW professionals had tried for weeks and failed.

The labor board limited the union to seven organizers inside the camp. "We went in with guitars," Luis told me. "No hard sell or promises of gross income or anything like that; just songs about ourselves—the workers—and about Mexican folk heroes, or about a Mexican-American boy killed in Vietnam. We try to interest people in their own dignity—not in violent revolution, but in racial pride, and the necessity for Chicanos to be proud people. Then, when they begin to understand that they're people, not animals, you can talk about how the union is part of this peaceful revolution, and how it can help everybody."

And that, Luis said, is where the success of the theater lies. "If we can get a couple of hundred people to watch us, then we're doing all right. Sure, we have success in colleges, and when we go out fund-raising. And things worked out well when we played in the courtyard of the Senate in Washington, D.C. But really, the best feeling comes when we play to a Chicano audience, and they see us, and like us, and talk about us, and maybe want to start a new teatro of their own."

Which, I guess, is the best way to feel. What I learned today, about the Teatro's history and goals, makes me want to stay longer here in Fresno. It's almost as if Luis was breathing new theatrical life into me. Maybe he is. All I know is that what he wants to do is right. I've looked at a couple of acto scripts, and I'm impressed. Tomorrow we start out early for Madera, about twenty-five miles north of here, where the Teatro's going to perform. It'll be the first time I've ever seen them in their milieu, and I'm godawful excited about it.

I'll let you know how it goes. Meanwhile, enjoy the enclosed acto.

Love,

j

LA QUINTA TEMPORADA

AN ACTO BY EL TEATRO CAMPESINO

Enter FARMWORKER *to center stage from S.L. He addresses* AUDIENCE.

FARMWORKER: Oh, hello—quehubole! My name is Jose . . . what else? . . . and I'm looking for a job. Do you have a job? I can do anything, any kind of field work. You see, I just got in from Texas this morning and I need to send money back to my familia. I can do whatever you want—pick cotton, grapes, melons.

(DON COYOTE *enters while* FARMWORKER *is talking. He smiles and comes toward the* FARMWORKER.)

DON COYOTE: My friend! My name is Don Coyote, and I am a farm labor contractor.

FARMWORKER: En la madre, me raye! Un contratista. (*The* FARMWORKER *kisses the* CONTRACTOR's *outstretched hand.*)

DON COYOTE: So you want work, eh? Busca jale? Bueno, véngase pa'ca un momento. (DON COYOTE *pulls* FARMWORKER *over to S.R.*) Mire—this summer is coming fat, *fat!* Covered with money! Dollar bills, five-dollar bills, ten, twenty, fifty, a hundred dollar bills and all you have to do is . . . (DON COYOTE *gestures above* FARMWORKER's *head as if holding a wad of money, which he now releases*) . . . catch!

(FARMWORKER *pretends to catch money in his hat.* DON COYOTE *moves downstage center.*)

DON COYOTE: Well, what do you say? Will you work for me?

FARMWORKER: Oh sí, patroncito! Sí, señor! (*Approaches* DON COYOTE, *hand out.*)

DON COYOTE (*grasping hand, shaking it*): A deal is a deal.

(*The* PATRONCITO *enters on S.R., stomps downstage smoking a cigar.*)

PATRÓN: Boy!

(DON COYOTE *shoves* FARMWORKER *aside and leaps toward the* GROWER, *landing at his feet and kissing his boots. He rises, dusting off the* PATRÓN.)

PATRÓN: Like your patrón, eh, boy?

DON COYOTE: Oh sí, patrón!

PATRÓN: Good. You got my summer crew ready, boy?

DON COYOTE: Sí, señor.

(*He motions to* FARMWORKER, *who hesitates, then comes over to* GROWER. DON COYOTE *points to the* FARMWORKER's *hat.*) El sombrero, babozo.

(*The* FARMWORKER *removes his hat and stands beside the* CONTRACTOR, *both smiling asininely toward the* GROWER.)

PATRÓN: Well, I don't much care what he looks like, so long as he can pick.

DON COYOTE: Oh, he can pick, patrón!

(*The* PATRÓN *stomps over to S.L.* DON COYOTE *elbows the* FARMWORKER *and makes a gesture, holding his hand widely apart as if describing how fat* SUMMER *will be. The* PATRÓN, *at S.L., calls in* SUMMER.)

PATRÓN: Summer! Get in here.

(SUMMER *is a man dressed in an ordinary workshirt and khaki hat. His shirt and hat, however, are completely covered with paper money: tens, twenties, fifties. He walks in with his arms outstretched, and continues across the stage at a normal pace.*)

SUMMER: I am Summer.

FARMWORKER: AJUA! El jale!

DON COYOTE: Éntrale, mano!

(*The* FARMWORKER *attacks the* SUMMER, *and begins to pick off as many dollar bills as his hands can grab. These he stuffs into his back pockets.* DON COYOTE *immediately takes his place behind the* FARMWORKER *and extracts the money from his back pockets, and hands*

LA QUINTA TEMPORADA 23

it over to the Patrón, *who has taken his place behind* Don Coyote. *This exchange continues until* Summer *exits. The* Patrón *then moves to S.R., counting his money.* Don Coyote *takes the* Farmworker *to S.L.*)

Don Coyote (*enthusiastically*): Te aventates! Didn't I tell you we're going to get rich? Didn't I tell you?

(Don Coyote *breaks off abruptly and goes over to his* Patrón's *side.*) How'd we do, boss?

Patrón: Terrible! We're going to have to ask for a federal subsidy.

(*The* Farmworker *searches his pockets for money and panics when he can't find a single dollar bill. He spots the* Grower *with handfuls of money, and his panic turns to anger.*)

Farmworker (*to* Don Coyote): Hey! Where's my money?

Don Coyote: What money?

Farmworker: Pos what? The money I work for all summer.

Don Coyote: You know what's wrong with you? You're stupid. You don't know how to *save* your money. Look at my patrón—how come he always has money?

Farmworker (*lunging toward* Patrón): That's *my* money!

Don Coyote (*stops him*): No! I know who has your money. Come here.

(*He takes* Farmworker *S.L. again.*) It's . . . (*He points out toward the* Audience, *making a semicircle from S.L. to S.R., finally stopping at the* Patrón *and pointing at him inadvertently.*)

Patrón: Hey!

Don Coyote: No! Not my patrón! It's Autumn! Autumn has your money.

Farmworker: Autumn?

Don Coyote: El Otoño.

Farmworker: Puras papas. I don't believe you.

Don Coyote: You don't believe me? (*faking his sincerity*) But I swear by my madrecita!

(*Pause.*)

Still don't believe me, eh? Okay. Do you want to see the truth in action? Well, here's the truth in action! (*He makes a flourish with his arm and spits on the floor, then stomps vigorously on the spit with his foot—all in a grandiose manner.*)

FARMWORKER: That's it?

DON COYOTE: La verdad en acción.

FARMWORKER: Well, here goes mine! (FARMWORKER *spits at* DON COYOTE's *foot, but* DON COYOTE *pulls it back just in time. He retaliates by spitting toward* FARMWORKER's *foot.* FARMWORKER *pulls his foot back just in time, as* DON COYOTE *stomps toward it. The* FARMWORKER *now catches* DON COYOTE *off guard by spitting in his face.*)

DON COYOTE (*retreats momentarily, decides to suppress his anger*): No matter. Look, mano, this autumn is coming *fat!* Fatter than last summer. You go to work for me and you'll be rich. You'll have enough money to buy yourself a new car, a Cadillac! Two Cadillacs! You'll have a house in the suburbs. You'll be able to go to Acapulco! Guadalajara! You'll be able to send your kids to college! You'll be able to afford a budget! You'll be middle-class! You'll be Anglo! You'll be rich!

(*The* FARMWORKER *responds to all of this with paroxysms of joy, squeals of delight.*)

DON COYOTE: So what do you say? Will you work for me?

FARMWORKER (*suddenly deadpan*): No.

DON COYOTE (*turns away, goes D.S.C.*): Okay. No me importa! I don't give a damn. Anyway, winter's coming.

FARMWORKER (*suddenly fearful*): Winter?

DON COYOTE: El invierno!

FARMWORKER: No! (*He rushes toward the* CONTRACTOR, *hand outstretched.* DON COYOTE *grabs it quickly, before the* FARMWORKER *can think twice.*)

DON COYOTE: Lío es lío, yo soy tu tío, grillo.

PATRÓN (*at S.R.*): Boy!

Don Coyote (*whirling around*): Yes, patrón?

Patrón (*stuffing money into his pockets*): Is my fall crew ready?

Don Coyote: Sí, patrón. (*He motions the* Farmworker *over to S.R. The* Farmworker *steps forward, hat in hand, with a smile on his face. The* Patrón *moves forward with a grunt, and the* Farmworker *steps in front of him. The* Patrón *tries to move around him, and the* Farmworker *moves in front of him again. The* Patrón *finally shoves the* Farmworker *aside and goes S.L.*)

Don Coyote (*to* Farmworker): Un lado, suato!

Patrón: Fall, come in here, boy.

(Fall *comes in. He is a thinner man than* Summer. *His workshirt is covered with money, though more sparsely than* Summer's.)

Don Coyote: Éntrale, mano!

(*With a shout, the* Farmworker *leaps to his work, picking money off the shirt that* Fall *wears. The same* Farmworker-Don Coyote-Patrón *arrangement is used until* Fall *is almost offstage at S.R. At this point, the* Farmworker *reaches back and accidentally catches* Don Coyote's *hand in his back pocket. Spotting this, the* Patrón *rapidly crosses to D.S.L.*)

Farmworker: Hey! That's my money! You're stealing my money! Pos mira, qué hijo de—

(*The* Farmworker *strikes at* Don Coyote, *who knocks him down and kicks him three times. The* Patrón *stands watching all of this, then finally calls out:*)

Patrón: You, boy!

Don Coyote (*in a sweat, fearful of reprimand*): Sí, patroncito? I didn't mean it, boss.

(*Pointing to his foot.*) Mira, rubber soles, patrón.

(Don Coyote *obsequiously sidles over to the* Patrón. *The* Patrón *is expansive, beaming, pleased.*)

Patrón: I like the way you do that, boy.

Don Coyote: You do? Oh, I can do it again, patrón. (*He runs over to the* FARMWORKER *and gives him one final kick in the ribs. The* FARMWORKER *groans.*)

PATRÓN (*with corporate pride*): Beautiful! If there's anything we need in our company, boy, it's discipline and control of our workers!

DON COYOTE: Sí, señor, disciplina, control de los Mexicans!

PATRÓN: And just to show you our appreciation for what you do for the business, the corporation, I am going to give you a little bonus.

(*Above the flat behind the* PATRÓN *and the* CONTRACTOR, *a hand appears holding a huge bone with big black letters spelling out the word "bonus." The* PATRÓN *picks this up and hands it to the* CON-TRACTOR.)

DON COYOTE (*overcome with emotion*): Oh, patrón! Un hueso!

(*There is a loud rumbling noise backstage. Snowflakes come tum-bling over the flats.*)

DON COYOTE (*running to S.R.*): Winter is coming!

(*The* FARMWORKER *picks himself up off the floor and cowers at U.S.C. The* PATRÓN *stands S.L., undisturbed by the advent of* WINTER. *With a final rumble* WINTER *leaps into the scene around the corner of the flat at S.L.*)

WINTER: I am Winter and I want money. Money for gas, lights, tele-phone, rent. (*He spots the* CONTRACTOR *and rushes over to him.*) Money!

(DON COYOTE *gives him his bonus.* WINTER *bites the bone, finds it distasteful, throws it backstage over the flats. He whirls around to-ward the* PATRÓN.) Money!

PATRÓN (*remaining calm*): Will you take a check?

WINTER (*rushing over to him*): No, cash!

PATRÓN: Okay, here! (*hands him a small wad of bills*)
    Well, that's it for me. I'm off to Acapulco 'til next spring. (*Exits S.L.*)

DON COYOTE: And I'm off to Las Vegas. (*Exits S.R.*)

FARMWORKER: And I'm off to eat frijoles!

(WINTER *nabs the* FARMWORKER *as he tries to escape.*)

WINTER: Ha, ha, Winter's got you! I want money! Give me money!

FARMWORKER: I don't have any. I'm just a poor farmworker.

WINTER: Then suffer! (WINTER *drags the* FARMWORKER *D.S.C., kicking and beating him, then dumps snow on him from a small pouch. The* FARMWORKER *shivers helplessly.* SPRING *enters at S.L., singing a happy tune.*)

SPRING (*skipping in*): La, la, la, la, la. (*Stops, sees* WINTER *maltreating* FARMWORKER.) What are *you* doing here?

WINTER: Mamasota, who are you?

SPRING: I am Spring, la primavera, but your time is past. You have to go!

WINTER: Some other time, baby.

SPRING: Aw, come on now, you've had your turn. You've got to leave.

(WINTER *ignores her with a grunt.*)

SPRING: Get the hell out of here!

WINTER: All right, I'm going for now, but I'll be back again next year, farmworker. Damn women! (*Exits S.R.*)

SPRING (*crosses to* FARMWORKER *and helps him to get up*): There, there, you poor, poor farmworker, here, now, get up. You mustn't let this happen to you again. You've got to fight for your rights!

FARMWORKER: You mean I've got rights?

SPRING: Sure!

FARMWORKER: Ahora, sí. I'm going to fight for my rights like Pancho Villa, like Francisco I. Madero, like Emiliano Zapa—

(SPRING *startles him by touching his shoulder.*) Ta-ta-ta!

(*From backstage is heard the cry: Campesino!*)

SPRING: Oh, my time has come . . . (*crosses in front of* FARMWORKER) I must go now. But remember, fight for your rights! La, la, la, la. (*Exits S.R., singing and skipping.*)

FARMWORKER: She's right! From now on I'm going to fight for my rights, my lefts, and my liberals.

(DON COYOTE *enters S.L.*)

DON COYOTE: Amigo—

FARMWORKER (*turns, frightened, runs to S.R. after* SPRING): Pri—

DON COYOTE: Pri, what?

FARMWORKER: Pri—prepare yourself! You robbed me!

DON COYOTE: No! No, I'm your friend.

FARMWORKER: NI MADRE! You're a thief!

DON COYOTE: No, soy tu amigo. Somos de la misma raza!

FARMWORKER: Simon, eres rata! (*He swings at* DON COYOTE.)

DON COYOTE: Calma, hombre! Ahí viene mi patrón!

FARMWORKER: Que venga ese cab—

PATRÓN (*enters S.L.*): Boy!

DON COYOTE (*rushing over to him*): Yes, boss?

PATRÓN: You got this year's summer crew ready?

DON COYOTE (*hesitating, hat in hand*): Well, you see, patrón, it's this way—

PATRÓN: Well?

DON COYOTE (*with a forced smile*): Sure, boss, it's all ready.

PATRÓN: Good!

(*He turns and crosses to corner of flat at S.L., anticipating the entrance of* SUMMER.)

(DON COYOTE *rushes to* FARMWORKER *at S.R.*)

DON COYOTE: Ándale, mano! You got to work. Haven't I always give you work? Don't I always treat you good?

FARMWORKER: No!

DON COYOTE: Ándale, hombre, be a sport! Do it for old times' sake!

FARMWORKER: No, te digo!

(*He spots* SUMMER *coming in at S.L.*) Estoy en *huelga!* (*He squats.*)

PATRÓN: What's going on? Why isn't he working?

DON COYOTE: He says he's on strike.

PATRÓN: STRIKE? But he can't be! Summer's going by! What does he want?

DON COYOTE (*to* FARMWORKER): Qué quieres?

FARMWORKER: Un contrato bien firmadito.

DON COYOTE: He wants a signed contract!

PATRÓN: He's crazy! We need some more workers! Find me some more workers! Summer's passing!

(*to audience*) Five hundred workers! I need five hundred workers!

(*Meanwhile,* SUMMER *continues to cross the stage and finally exits S.R. The* PATRÓN *is frantic, hysterical. He ends up following* SUMMER *offstage. There is a silence. The* PATRÓN *re-enters in shock and disbelief.*)

PATRÓN: He's gone. Summer's gone. My crop! Ahhhhhhhhhhh! (*He leaps and snorts like an animal.*)

DON COYOTE (*fearfully*): Patrón! Patrón!

(*The* PATRÓN *is on the floor, kicking and snorting like a wild horse.* DON COYOTE *leaps on his back and rides him like a bronco until the* PATRÓN *calms down and settles on all fours, snorting and slobbering incoherently.*)

DON COYOTE (*patting the side of his head like a horse*): Chihuahua, cada año se pone más animal, mi patrón. It's okay, boss. He can't last, because he's getting hungry. (FARMWORKER *doubles over with pangs of hunger.*)

And anyway, here comes Autumn! (AUTUMN *crosses the stage and the* FARMWORKER *approaches him with one hand on his stomach and his other arm outstretched.*)

FARMWORKER: Con esto me compro un taco.

DON COYOTE (*slapping his hand down*): None of that! Put it here first! (*Stretches out his hand.*)

FARMWORKER: No, I can't, I'm on strike!

DON COYOTE: No work, no eat! Put it here!

FARMWORKER: No, I—(*He hesitates. He is almost ready to take the* CONTRACTOR'S *hand.*)

(SPRING *enters S.L. dressed as a nun representing the Churches.*)

CHURCHES: Wait! (*crosses to* FARMWORKER) I am the Churches. I bring you food and money. (*She hands him some cash and fruit.*)

PATRÓN (*back to his senses*): You—you lousy contractor! You lost me my summer crop and my fall crop. You're fired! And you, you Communist farmworker—(*points to* NUN)—You too, you Catholic Communist!

(*A rumbling noise backstage.*)

(*The* FARMWORKER *is frightened. He tries to run but the* NUN *holds him. The* PATRÓN *cowers U.S.C.* SUMMER *enters dressed as "unions" and carries a contract and an oversized pencil.*)

UNIONS (*D.S.C.*): I am the Unions. We're with you, brother! Keep fighting! (*Crosses to* FARMWORKER *and shakes his hand and stands by his side.*)

(*There is another rumbling noise backstage.*)

(FALL *re-enters dressed as a Mexican revolutionary representing "la raza."*)

LA RAZA: La Raza está contigo, mano. Sigue luchando. (*He also joins the ranks around the* FARMWORKER.)

(*One final gigantic rumble from backstage.*)

(*With snow spilling over the flats, then* WINTER *enters with a vengeance.*)

WINTER: "Llego el lechero!" And my name ain't Granny Goose, baby! Money, give me money! (*He charges toward the* FARMWORKER *and is repulsed by the* CHURCHES, LA RAZA, *and the* UNIONS, *who shout "NO!"*)

WINTER: That's what I like, spunk! (*He tries again and is repulsed a second time.*) God damn!!!

(*He tries one final time, making himself as big and as frightening as possible, but he fails again. He asks them:*) Who has money?

(*The* CHURCHES, *the* UNIONS, *and* LA RAZA *point at the* PATRÓN *and shout: "He has." With a gleeful shout,* WINTER *assails the* PATRÓN, *demanding money. The* PATRÓN *pulls out money from all of his pockets, wads and wads of it, until he runs out.*)

WINTER: More!

PATRÓN: That's all I have.

WINTER: More!

PATRÓN: I don't have any more. Except what I have in the bank.

(*With a savage look in his eye,* WINTER *takes a step backward and gets ready to leap at the* PATRÓN's *throat. The* PATRÓN *is transfixed with fear. He is unable to move until* WINTER *grabs him by the throat and drags him D.S.C.*)

PATRÓN: But I don't have any money.

WINTER: Then freeze to death! (WINTER *kicks and beats the* PATRÓN *and pours snow all over him. The* PATRÓN *shivers and looks up toward the* CHURCHES, *the* UNIONS, *and* LA RAZA.)

PATRÓN: Help me!

UNIONS, LA RAZA, CHURCHES: Sign a contract!

FARMWORKER: Firma un contrato!

PATRÓN (*after a pause*): Go to hell!

(*The* CHURCHES, *the* UNIONS, *and* LA RAZA *turn their backs on the* PATRÓN. WINTER *continues to drop snow on the* PATRÓN.)

WINTER (*singing*): I'm dreaming of a white Christmas—(*more snow*). If only Santa could see me now.

PATRÓN: Help me!

UNIONS, LA RAZA, CHURCHES: SIGN A CONTRACT!!!

FARMWORKER: Firma un contrato!!!

PATRÓN (*after a pause*): All right!

(*The* UNIONS *hand the* FARMWORKER *the contract and the pencil. The* FARMWORKER *comes forward and hands them to the* PATRÓN. *In panic,* DON COYOTE *comes around and kneels beside his boss.*)

DON COYOTE: No, patrón, don't sign! I'll be out of a job. I brought you wetbacks. They're Communists. Noooooo!

(*The* PATRÓN *signs the contract and hands it to the* FARMWORKER, *who looks at it in disbelief.*)

FARMWORKER: Two dollars an hour . . . rest rooms in the fields . . . vacations with pay . . . GANAMOS!!!

(*The* FARMWORKER's *supporters give out a cheer and pick him up on their shoulders and carry him out triumphantly. The* PATRÓN *crawls out on his hands and knees in the opposite direction.* DON COYOTE *tries to sneak out with the crowd, but* WINTER *catches him.*)

WINTER: Ah-hah! Winter's got you!

DON COYOTE (*bluffing*): Winter? Hah! Winter's already past! (WINTER *slaps his forehead stupidly.* DON COYOTE *laughs and starts to walk out. Then suddenly* WINTER *snaps his fingers as if realizing something.*)

WINTER: The fifth season! I'm the fifth season!

DON COYOTE: What fifth season? There are only four!

WINTER (*tearing off the top layer of the sign hanging from his neck, revealing a new sign underneath*): La justicia social!

DON COYOTE: Social justice? Oh, no! (WINTER *kicks* DON COYOTE *offstage, then turns toward the audience.*)

WINTER: Si alguien pregunta que pasó con ese contratista chueco, díganle que se lo llevó la quinta chin—LA QUINTA TEMPORADA!!!

(*Exits S.L.*)

Dear Nancy

The heat again. The damn heat. It creates a thirst in me like I've never had before. I traveled up here, about twenty miles north of Fresno, with the Teatro this morning. By ten, when we left, it was so hot that my tape recorder seized up and I've had to take notes all the way, in the bumpy-riding panel truck that holds the portable stage, the prop trunks, and about six of the Teatro members. The truck is not new, and its bumpers are plastered with HUELGA and BOYCOTT GRAPES stickers. There's a UFW flag—the red background and black eagle—flying from the radio antenna, and the inside, until the windows were rolled down, was blue with Luis' cigar smoke.

Today was my first exposure to the Teatro in what I like to think of romantically as battle conditions. We got to Madera by eleven-thirty and drove around the barrio, with loudspeakers inside the trucks calling the people out to see the performance, held in a park right by the town's civic swimming pool. It was the first time I could see what Luis meant when he said that although the Teatro wasn't physically assaulted, as it had been during the Delano days, there are still a lot of hassles between the Chicanos and the authorities.

It took an hour and a half to set up the portable stage—the first time that the company has used it. From now on it'll take less time. We had to set up on concrete, although there was a lush patch of grass and trees, because the cops said Luis didn't have the right kind of permit for the grass. The concrete, needless to say, was hot enough to fry eggs on. And setting up on the concrete, we were right across from the swimming pool, with all the attendant noise that goes with it.

The heat was just abominable. An asphalt driveway—running around the park between the concrete where the stage was set up and the swimming pool—was so hot as to be mushy and sticky. And as if by mechanical design, a police cruiser with two riot-helmeted cops and their paraphernalia—shotguns (two), chemical Mace (two cans each), and cigars—made slow sweeps of the area. Never saying anything, but making everybody—myself included—nervous with their presence. I've never had a feeling like that before. The cops were there to harass the Teatro, and for no other reason. Which caused me to do some thinking.

The gathering was obviously peaceful. The stage was going up, and along with it the Teatro banners—brown and yellow rectangles, with Aztec designs hand-painted on them, which the troupe uses as their permanent backdrop, acto "curtain," and omnipresent advertising whenever they put on a show. The people who showed up early to watch the setup—mainly young kids, drawn by the long-haired Bronces and the pageantry of the whole idea of a Sunday of live theater—were definitely not out to cause any trouble. And still, the cops showed up. Not in force—just that one cruiser—but visibly enough for us to wonder what their motives were.

More frighteningly, there wasn't any communication between the Teatro and the Madera police. Luis wasn't about to make the first move—his permits were in order, and everything had been set up in advance—and the cops never said a word. They just cruised round and round the park, their wide-track tires making wide-track marks in the ever-softening asphalt, smoking their cigars, and watching. Watching.

The only obvious thing that Luis did was to tell his company and the onlookers to stay cool. We were thirsty, but we drank Cokes instead of beer. We used the wastebaskets and kept the place neat.

"I know," Luis nodded at the patrol car, "that if the Man tries to get us, it'll be on something like littering, or walking on the grass, or drinking beer on Madera city property, marijuana, or something similar, so we stay very clean. We don't even drink beer when we perform, and there's never any dope around. And that goes for the Centro in Fresno, too. We're part of the community. People look up to us, so there's an image to live up to. If there were dope, illicit sex, or drinking, we couldn't hold our people's respect for a minute. They come to us for help because they know we're straight."

Augustin Vera, guitarist and actor as well as technical director, strolled around with a massive toy rifle. "When we played the Senate," he said, "the pigs took this gun apart four times. And even then we had to shove Kleenex in the breach so they could see that it was only a toy. And man, it has a solid wooden barrel." He aimed the rifle toward the cruising police car. "Blan! Blan! Blan!"

"Cool it, man." Luis waved him down. "We can't afford trouble, Augustin. It's taken us too long to set up the stage." He shrugged.

"They'll just take it as an excuse to close us down. It's pressure, but we have to take it."

The Teatro is always under pressure—from the police, labor contractors, the vintners, and even from the Teamsters, who, two years ago, tried to organize the California agricultural workers into their organization, instead of the AFL-CIO UFW, but failed miserably due to the efforts of Cesar Chavez and Luis Valdez and the Teatro.

Luis admits that there are still occasional threats directed at the Teatro. "When the labor boys start to heckle us, though, we're surrounded by our own people, so they won't try anything. And all we want to do is perform, to do our thing so people can enjoy themselves."

Luis is the consummate *régisseur*. In his straw hat—the farmer's hat with a wide brim, his cigar clamped at a rakish angle in his mouth, sweat pouring from his underarms, soaking his back, he directed the technical people as they put up the set, marked positions for the prop boxes, tuned guitars, sent out for Cokes and sandwiches, and mapped out the routes for the sound trucks to follow in their second circuits of the barrio, to bring people out to the show.

By about one o'clock the stage work was finished. The raked platform looked great—painted in red and brown, with the backdrop up, flapping in a hot wind. It was like a classic Spanish stage, or a Renaissance troupe of merry mummers, come to set up in an inn courtyard. A festive, comfortable feeling. I was strangely at home among the Bronces, whose language I don't speak and whose culture I'm unfamiliar with. Still, there was a universality about the whole thing that put me at ease. Much of that feeling is due to Luis, who for some strange reason has taken a liking to me. Or perhaps it's that I worked with the Teatro, helping them put up the stage.

The Teatro's host organization, the California Rural Legal Assistance Fund, had crates of melons (union-picked, of course), which they handed out to the audience as they arrived. The joy of a vine-fresh melon, sliced with a machete and eaten with the hands, is completely ineffable.

Finally (by about two o'clock) things started. The crowd was about 150, maybe a few more. But people kept dribbling in. According to Luis, it wasn't a bad turnout. "Average" is the way he put it.

I got to speak to Carlos Ynostroza, a counsel for the CRLA and one of the sponsors of the Madera performance, just before the show started. His reaction to the Teatro was, I gather, characteristic. "We asked El Teatro here," said Ynostroza, "because they can create the pride in being Mexican that it's so important to have. El Teatro makes us laugh at ourselves. But at the same time, it forces us all to be aware of where we stand with the white power structure that's so prevalent in the valley. And they show us how far we're going to have to go to claim our self-respect and racial pride.

"Also, Luis and the Teatro state the message of organization very effectively. I mean people can *see* right before them why the union is a good thing, and why it's important not to fold early in the game. You sit through *La Quinta Temporada* and you see faces not only smiling because the play is funny, but nodding in agreement, because the workers know what's happening. Money is *like* that to them. The contractor is *like* that to them. The boss is *like* that to them. And they see. They understand. Maybe they'll see that the union is like El Teatro says it is. Or that a contract is important for their own well-being.

"Maybe they'll even join the union. Not the first time, perhaps, but after the second time they see the Teatro. Luis and the Teatro make my people *think,* which is something no one has done in a long time."

Ynostroza's reaction to the Teatro is shared by most Chicanos who realize that the pragmatic approach of the Teatro constitutes a political reality, able to coerce change from people who have endured the same conditions for more than two generations.

And Luis, who begins every performance with a speech, knows how to gauge his audience. He talks simply: "We are El Teatro Campesino de Fresno," he begins. "The Farmworkers' Theater." He tells them that the Teatro has played in Madera before, when Cesar Chavez marched from Delano to Sacramento to plead the cause of the UFW directly with the California legislators—a long, hot, dusty march that wound through the fields and towns of rural California and ended on the steps of the state capitol.

"You know," he says, "there have got to be some changes for the Chicano. We are a proud race of people—descended from kings. We need to maintain our self-respect. Here. Now. In the fields, in the towns—los pueblos—and all through our land."

His eyes scan the audience. He searches among the people for understanding. There are few who agree or understand. One man walks up to the edge of the stage and drunkenly leans on it. He looks at Valdez and the members of the Teatro. "Do you want a fight now?" he asks in Spanish. "Do you want to fight? 'Cause I'll fight now." Two men walk to him and he is escorted through the crowd.

"I don't want to fight now," Luis calls after the man. "I want to regain my pride, and not become part of a society I don't understand and that doesn't understand me." He comes back to the audience.

"What we say here in Madera today is for you to see yourselves as you are; to see the need for education, but not to become part of the system; to become a proud and emancipated people.

"You know, I was almost taken in by the system a few years ago, when I lived in Delano, not far from here. I was going to school, and we were poor, my family, like you. And I took my lunch wrapped in newspaper—tacos and beans. You know? So one day I looked at my white classmates, and they weren't eating tacos and beans. They were eating bread. White, spongy bread. With stuff on it. And they were wearing nice clothes and stuff, and all of a sudden my taco didn't look very good any more. I didn't want the taco. I wanted a sandwich, with white bread and good things like peanut butter, or bologna, or processed cheese. You know, all those good things. We didn't have money, really, but my mother went out and bought white bread and bologna, oh, and waxed paper, because if we took sandwiches wrapped in newspaper it would have blown the whole thing, you know? Anyhow, there I was, eating white bread sandwiches wrapped in waxed paper in school, and tacos at home. And I felt guilty about the tacos because I liked them more than I liked white bread.

"And that's the way we're all sucked into the system, wanting things because they're acceptable, and our things aren't. But we have to get to know ourselves. We have to be aware that we are descended from a race of kings. From kings! And we're proud people, who have to regain our pride in la raza, la raza that we're a part of. And that's what I want us to fight for—our raza—our acceptance as human beings. For acceptance as ourselves.

Luis is a forceful speaker, and a coaxing one, too. He makes sense to his audience, speaking a mixture of English and Spanish. But it's an altogether different technique than he uses when he's talking to a white audience. I remember seeing the Teatro for the first time in Los Angeles, at the Greek Theater, when they performed in an antiwar benefit. Luis talked, I recall, for about fifteen minutes, and his language was from the streets, not the soapbox.

"We're not happy here," I remember him shouting. "I mean by that, we can't take time to fuck around trying to show you people what our revolution is all about. Our people, my people, understand the revolution instinctively, because we've been taking it up the ass for two hundred years or more. The Teatro is here today because you're paying us expenses, and the money you're raising goes to help the Los Angeles Chicano community—the less Bronces die in the Nam, the better for us and our community here. But that's why we're here. We don't belong here, though, we belong in the fields with the workers. They get fucked every day in the ass because they won't fight back. Well, the Teatro's here to show them *how* to fight back.

"And you can't buy us off with dinero—money—you know we don't take grants any more. We want the land back, and power, and guns to protect ourselves if necessary, and we'll fight to take them if we have to. We are la raza nueva, and we plan to prove that with action, not just words."

A great difference between the Greek Theater and Madera. Both were in the sun, on hot afternoons. But that's where the similarity stopped.

Luis says, though, "you gotta be pragmatic. Students and hip whites know we're angry, and they expect radical talk from us. Maybe it soothes them, or helps them to justify us. I'm not sure at all. What I do know is that when we perform for liberal audiences, they've come to expect the classic brown power harangue, and I'm happy to give it to them if it'll make them feel better.

"Now, young Bronces are another thing altogether. They expect the radical talk because that's what they believe in. Chicano college students are into power politics and confrontationism. But for the workers? No. It doesn't do anything for them or us. As a matter of fact, it would hurt both us and the union if we did that kind of thing in front of them. I mean, there are a lot of Chicano mothers who would get very upset if they heard a Bronce kid like me speaking in public and using the word 'fuck.' "

Pragmatic is the word, without a doubt. But if Luis' speeches differ, the actos are constant. They get the same responses no matter what the culture of the audience.

Actos are so simple as to be maddening. They're brilliant—no other word will do. Pared down to the bones, comedic as Abbott and Costello or the Marx Brothers, they're a mixture of circus and politics, clowning and pathos. And simple. That's the key word.

Los Vendidos (*The Sellouts*) is an excellent example. The scene is "Sancho's Used Mexican Lot." There are three models on the showroom floor, all denoted by signs: Farmworker, Pachuco (city-bred Chicano) and Revolucionario. The props and costumes are simple: ragged clothes and big sombrero for the farmworker, satin shirt and switchblade knife for the Pachuco, and carbine, serapi, and ammunition bandillero for the revolutionary. Valdez plays "Honest Sancho," with all the aplomb of a smooth-talking used-car salesman.

The plot is simple. A woman from the governor's office comes to buy an acceptable Mexican to be shown off as part of an "integrated" government. She is shown the three models but rejects them: the worker because he is dirty and speaks no English, the Pachuco because he curses at her and steals her pocketbook, and the revolutionary because he is too violent. Then Sancho brings out his "newest model," the acclimated Mexican-American, wearing a suit and tie. It speaks carefully polished phrases. This model runs on Mom's apple pie, bologna sandwiches, and dry martinis, although, Sancho admits, it eats Mexican food on ceremonial occasions.

The woman buys the Mexican-American model, but as soon as she has paid her money, it goes berserk, shouting "Viva La Huelga! Viva La Raza!" and with the other "used Mexicans," chases her off-stage. The characters come back, divide up the money, and carry off Honest Sancho, who is in reality a robot, to be serviced.

Both student and worker audiences get the same thing out of the play: that even the most accepted Mexican-American is still basically a Mexican, and has his heritage to consider before he sells out his own people. But whereas the older workers nod in agreement, activists and students stomp and cheer, catcalling at the government woman and yelling insults at her. "They see," says Luis, "that their heritage has been attacked by the white man."

The Teatro is proud of its center, because it's in constant use by the community. The Chicanos are beginning to recognize the significance of the use of culture—music, theater, and all the folk arts —as a way of maintaining their spirit and even their militancy.

Which is something that's come about mainly since 1967, when the Teatro broke away from the UFW. At first, the Teatro was strictly an organizing arm for Cesar Chavez's union. But unionizing by itself left Luis without any real far-reaching goals. Hence the whole cultural awareness message, and the Teatro's use of historicity —themes like Joaquin, *Vietnam Campesino, Soldato Razo,* and *The Shrunken Head of Pancho Villa*—to enforce a feeling of pride in the audience, as well as to reinforce their cultural and linguistic background.

Now that the state of California is "enlightened" and it's not improper to have bilingual schools in Chicano areas, the things that Luis has been preaching since 1965 are accepted more and more by educators and establishment people. Maybe the best thing about what Luis is doing, though, is that he's doing it without relying on funding except through his performances. That way he keeps his nose clean: he owes nothing to anyone. And even though the company members only get about sixty dollars a month—which is roughly the equivalent of striker's pay—the theater exists, and does some of the most powerful stuff I've seen in a long time.

I guess that people are becoming much more aware of the Chicano heritage here in California. The theater I'm off to next—the Teatro's second permanent theater in San Juan Bautista—is the result of one guy's acceptance of his Chicano heritage, and his need to help other people achieve the same level of awareness he has.

I'm excited about going to San Juan Bautista, because the company, which is headed by Luis' brother, Daniel, is much younger than the one here in Fresno. They're mainly young students, formerly in Daniel's El Teatro Urbano, which came out of San Jose State College. And they have a Centro Cultural in what used to be one of the most prestigious Mexican towns in California. Now, from what I gather, there's a mission and a lot of curio shops. But the heritage is there. And, more exciting, Daniel Valdez told me that there was a chance that the Teatro from San Juan Bautista will do a show at Soledad Prison; and not in the auditorium, but inside the lockup—in the library, which is next to the Adjustment Center, where the Soledad Brothers used to be held.

The feelings I'm having are exhilarating, to say the least. After yesterday in Fresno and today in Madera, I'm beginning to regain my faith in theater as a practicable, effective, social form of communication among people.

The audience reaction to the actos, even in the heat—that hot, stultifying heat—was tremendous. They knew what Luis and the company was all about, and they knew that what they saw was honest, truly people's theater.

There was so much life to the way the audience shouted "Viva La Raza!" that one couldn't help but believe that the Teatro had started to change their lives. Not a whole lot, but a start.

I'm enclosing one of the Teatro's actos, plus an article by Luis. Please put them aside.

More from San Juan Bautista soon.

Love,
j

LOS VENDIDOS

AN ACTO BY EL TEATRO CAMPESINO

SCENE: *Honest Sancho's Used Mexican Lot and Mexican Curio Shop. Three models are on display in Honest Sancho's Shop. To the right there is a* REVOLUCIONARIO, *complete with sombrero, carrillares, and carabina 30-30. At center, on the floor, there is the* FARMWORKER, *sleeping under a broad straw sombrero. At stage left is the* JOHNNY PACHUCO, *filero in hand.* HONEST SANCHO *is moving among his models, dusting them off and preparing for another day of business.*

SANCHO: Bueno, bueno, mis monos, vamos a ver a quien vendemos ahara, no?

(*To audience*): Quehubo! I'm Honest Sancho and this is my shop. Antes fui contratista pero ahora pero ahora legre tener mi negocio. All I need now is a customer. . . . (*A bell rings offstage.*) Ay, a customer!

(*Entering.*)

SECRETARY: Good morning, I'm Miss Jimenez from—

SANCHO: Ah, una chicana! Welcome, welcome, Señorita Jimenez.

SECRETARY (*Anglo pronunciation*): JIM-enez.

SANCHO: Qué?

SECRETARY: My name is Miss JIM-enez. Don't you speak English? What's wrong with you?

SANCHO: Oh, nothing, Señorita JIM-enez. I'm here to help you.

SECRETARY: That's better. As I was starting to say, I'm a secretary from Governor Reagan's office, and we're looking for a Mexican type for the administration.

SANCHO: Well, you come to the right place, lady. This is Honest

Sancho's Used Mexican lot, and we got all the types here. Any particular type you want?

SECRETARY: Yes, we were looking for somebody suave. . . .

SANCHO (*Mexican pronunciation*): Suavé.

SECRETARY: Debonair.

SANCHO: De buen aire.

SECRETARY: Dark.

SANCHO: Priete.

SECRETARY: But of course not too dark.

SANCHO: No muy priete.

SECRETARY: Perhaps, beige.

SANCHO: Beige, just the tone. Así como cafecite con leche, no?

SECRETARY: One more thing. He must be hard-working.

SANCHO: That could only be one model. Step right over here to the center of the shop, lady.

(*They cross to the* FARMWORKER.) This is our standard farmworker model. As you can see, in the words of our beloved Senator George Murphy, he is "built close to the ground." Also take special notice of his four-ply Goodyear huaraches, made from the rain tire. This wide-brimmed sombrero is an extra-added feature . . . keeps off the sun, rain, and dust.

SECRETARY: Yes, it does look durable.

SANCHO: And our farmworker model is friendly. Muy amable. Watch. (*Snaps his fingers.*)

FARMWORKER (*lifts his head*): Buenos días, señorita (*his head drops*).

SECRETARY: My, he's friendly.

SANCHO: Didn't I tell you? Loves his patrones! But his most attractive feature is that he's hard-working. Let me show you. (*Snaps fingers.* FARMWORKER *stands.*)

FARMWORKER: El jale! (*He begins to work.*)

SANCHO: As you can see, he is cutting grapes.

SECRETARY: Oh? I wouldn't know.

SANCHO: He also picks cotton. (*Snap.* FARMWORKER *begins to pick cotton.*)

SECRETARY: Versatile, isn't he?

SANCHO: He also picks melons. (*Snap.* FARMWORKER *picks melons.*) That's his slow speed for late in the season. Here's his fast speed. (*Snap.* FARMWORKER *picks faster.*)

SECRETARY: Chihuaha—I mean, goodness, he sure is a hard worker.

SANCHO (*pulling the* FARMWORKER *to his feet*): And that isn't the half of it. Do you see these little holes on his arms that appear to be pores? During those hot, sluggish days in the field when the vines or the branches get so entangled, it's almost impossible to move, these holes emit a certain grease that allows our model to slip and slide right through the crop with no trouble at all.

SECRETARY: Wonderful. But is he economical?

SANCHO: Economical! Señorita, you are looking at the Volkswagen of Mexicans. Pennies a day is all it takes. One plate of beans and tortillas will keep him going all day. That, and chile. Plenty of chile. Jalapeños, chile verde, chile colorado. But, of course, if you do give him chile (*Snap.* FARMWORKER *turns left face.* *Snap.* FARMWORKER *bends over.*) . . . then you have to change his oil filter once a week.

SECRETARY: What about storage?

SANCHO: No problem. You know those new farm labor camps our honorable Governor Reagan has built by Parlior or Raisin City? They were designed with our model in mind. Five, six, seven, even ten in one of those shacks will give you no trouble at all. You can also put him in old barns, old cars, riverbanks. You can even leave him out in the field overnight with no worry!

SECRETARY: Remarkable.

SANCHO: And here's an added feature: Every year at the end of the season, this model goes back to Mexico and doesn't return, automatically, until next spring.

SECRETARY: How about that. But tell me, does he speak English?

SANCHO: Another outstanding feature is that last year this model was programmed to go out on STRIKE! (*Snap.*)

FARMWORKER: HUELGA! HUELGA! Hermanos, sálganse de esos files. (*Snap. He stops.*)

SECRETARY: No! Oh no, we can't strike in the state Capitol.

SANCHO: Well, he also scabs. (*Snap.*)

FARMWORKER: Yo me vendo barato. (*Snap.*)

SECRETARY: That's much better, but you didn't answer my question. Does he speak English?

SANCHO: Bueno . . . no, pero he has other—

SECRETARY: No.

SANCHO: —other features.

SECRETARY: *No!* He just won't do!

SANCHO: Okay, okay pues. We have other models.

SECRETARY: I hope so. What we need is something a little more sophisticated.

SANCHO: Sophisti—qué?

SECRETARY: An urban model.

SANCHO: Ah, from the city! Step right back. Over here in this corner of the shop is exactly what you're looking for. Introducing our new 1972 Johnny Pachuco model. This is our fastback model. Streamlined. Built for speed, low-riding, city life. Take a look at some of these features. Mag shoes, dual exhausts, green chartreuse paint job, dark-tint windshield, a little poof on top. Let me just turn him on. (*Snap.* JOHNNY PACHUCO *walks to stage center with a Pachuco bounce.*)

SECRETARY: What was that?

SANCHO: That, señorita, was the Chicano shuffle.

SECRETARY: Okay, what does he do?

SANCHO: Anything and everything necessary for city life. For instance, survival; he knife fights. (*Snap.* JOHNNY PACHUCO *pulls out switchblade and swings at* SECRETARY. *She screams.*)

SANCHO: He dances. (*Snap.*)

JOHNNY (*singing*): "Angel baby, my angel baby—" (*Snap.*)

SANCHO: And here's a feature no city model can be without. He gets arrested, but not without resisting, of course. (*Snap.*)

JOHNNY PACHUCO: En la madre, la place. I din't do it! I din't do it! (JOHNNY *turns and stands up against an imaginary wall, legs spread out, arms, as if handcuffed, behind his back.*)

SECRETARY: Oh no, we can't have arrests!

SANCHO: But he's bilingual!

SECRETARY: Bilingual!

SANCHO: Simon qué yes. He speaks English! Johnny, give us some English. (*Snap.*)

JOHNNY PACHUCO (*comes downstage*): Fuck you!

SECRETARY (*gasps*): Oh! I've never been so insulted in my whole life!

SANCHO: Well, he learned it in your school.

SECRETARY: I don't care where he learned it.

SANCHO: But he's economical!

SECRETARY: Economical?

SANCHO: Nickels and dimes. You can keep Johnny running on hamburgers, Taco Bell tacos, Lucky Lager beer, Thunderbird wine, yesca . . .

SECRETARY: Yesca?

SANCHO: Mota.

SECRETARY: Mota?

SANCHO: Zenos . . . MARIJUANA. (*Snap.* JOHNNY PACHUCO *inhales on an imaginary joint.*)

SECRETARY: That's against the law!

JOHNNY PACHUCO (*big smile, holding his breath*): Yeah.

SANCHO: He also sniffs glue. (*Snap.* JOHNNY PACHUCO *inhales glue, big smile.*)

JOHNNY PACHUCO: Tha's too man, *ese.*

SECRETARY: No, Mr. Sancho, I don't think this . . .

SANCHO: Wait a minute, he has other qualities I know you'll love. For example, an inferiority complex. (*Snap.*)

JOHNNY PACHUCO (*to* SANCHO): You think you're better than me, huh ese? (*Swings switchblade.*)

SANCHO: He can also be beaten and he bruises, cut and he bleeds, kicked and he . . . (*He beats, bruises, and kicks* JOHNNY PACHUCO) . . . would you like to try it?

SECRETARY: Oh, I couldn't.

SANCHO: Be my guest. He makes a great scapegoat.

SECRETARY: No, really.

SANCHO: Please.

SECRETARY: Well, all right. Just once. (*She kicks* JOHNNY PACHUCO.) Oh, he's so soft.

SANCHO: Wasn't that good? Try again.

SECRETARY (*kicks* JOHNNY PACHUCO): Oh, how nice. (*She kicks him again.*)

SANCHO: Okay, that's enough, lady. You'll ruin the merchandise. Yes, our Johnny Pachuco model can give you many hours of pleasure. Why, the LAPD just bought twenty of these to train their rookie cops on. And talk about maintenance. Señorita, you are looking at an entirely self-supporting machine. You're never going to find our Johnny Pachuco model on the relief rolls. No, sir, this model knows how to liberate.

SECRETARY: Liberate?

SANCHO: He steals. (*Snap.* JOHNNY PACHUCO *rushes the* SECRETARY *and steals her purse.*)

JOHNNY PACHUCO: Dame esa bolsa, vieja! (*He grabs the purse and runs. Snap by* SANCHO. *He stops.* SECRETARY *runs after* JOHNNY PACHUCO *and grabs purse away from him, kicking him as she goes.*)

SECRETARY: No, no, no! We can't have any more thieves in the state Administration. Put him back.

SANCHO: Okay, we still got other models. Come on, Johnny, we'll sell you to some old lady. (SANCHO *takes* JOHNNY PACHUCO *back to his place.*)

SECRETARY: Mr. Sancho, I don't think you quite understand what we need. What we need is something that will attract the women voters. Something more traditional, more romantic.

SANCHO: Ah, a lover. (*He smiles meaningfully.*) Step right over here, señorita. Introducing our standard Revolucionario and/or Early American Bandit type. As you can see, he is well-built, sturdy, durable. This is the International Harvester of Mexicans.

SECRETARY: What does he do?

SANCHO: You name, he does it. He rides horses, stays in the mountains, crosses deserts, plains, rivers, leads revolutions, follows revolutions, kills, can be killed, serves as a martyr, hero, movie star— did I say movie star? Did you ever see *Viva Zapata? Viva Villa, Villa Rides, Pancho Villa Returns, Pancho Villa Goes Back, Pancho Villa Meets Abbott and Costello* . . .

SECRETARY: I've never seen any of those.

SANCHO: Well, he was in all of them. Listen to this. (*Snap.*)

REVOLUCIONARIO (*scream*): VIVA VILLAAAA!

SECRETARY: That's awfully loud.

SANCHO: He has volume control. (*He adjusts volume. Snap.*)

REVOLUCIONARIO (*mousey voice*): Viva Villa.

SECRETARY: That's better.

SANCHO: And even if you didn't see him in the movies, perhaps you saw him on TV. He makes commercials. (*Snap.*)

REVOLUCIONARIO: Is there a Frito Bandito in *your* house?

SECRETARY: Oh, yes, I've seen that one!

SANCHO: Another feature about this one is that he is economical. He runs on raw horsemeat and tequila!

SECRETARY: Isn't that rather savage?

SANCHO: Al contrario, it makes him a lover. (*Snap.*)

REVOLUCIONARIO (*to* SECRETARY): Ay, mamacita, cochota, ven pa' aca! (*He grabs* SECRETARY *and folds her back, Latin lover style.*)

SANCHO (*Snap.* REVOLUCIONARIO *goes back upright*): Now, wasn't that nice?

SECRETARY: Well, it was rather nice.

SANCHO: And finally, there is one outstanding feature about this model I *know* the ladies are going to love; he's a genuine antique! He was made in Mexico in 1910!

SECRETARY: Made in Mexico?

SANCHO: That's right. Once in Tijuana, twice in Guadalajara, three times in Cuernavaca.

SECRETARY: Mr. Sancho, I thought he was an American product.

SANCHO: No, but—

SECRETARY: No, I'm sorry. We can't buy anything but American-made products. He just won't do.

SANCHO: But he's an antique!

SECRETARY: I don't care. You still don't understand what we need. It's true we need Mexican models such as these, but it's more important that he be *American*.

SANCHO: American?

SECRETARY: That's right, and judging from what you've shown me, I don't think you have what we want. Well, my lunch hour's almost over, I better . . .

SANCHO: Wait a minute! Mexican but American.

SECRETARY: That's correct.

SANCHO: Mexican but . . . (*a sudden flash*) . . . American! Yeah, I think we've got exactly what you want. He just came in today! Give me a minute.

(*He exits. Talks from backstage*): Here he is in the shop. Let me just get some papers off. There. Introducing our new 1973 Mexican-American! Ta-ra-ra-ra-ra-RA-RAA!

(SANCHO *brings out the* MEXICAN-AMERICAN *model, a clean-shaven middle-class type in a business suit, with glasses.*)

SECRETARY (*impressed*): Where have you been hiding this one?

SANCHO: He just came in this morning. Ain't he a beauty? Feast your eyes on him! Sturdy U. S. Steel frame, streamlined, modern. As a matter of fact, he is built exactly like our Anglo models except that he comes in a variety of darker shades: Naugahide, leather, or leatherette.

SECRETARY: Naugahide.

SANCHO: Well, we'll just write that down. Yes, señorita, this model represents the apex of American engineering. He is bilingual, college-educated, ambitious, say the word "acculturate," and he accelerates. He is intelligent, well-mannered, clean—did I say clean? (*Snap.* MEX-AM *raises his arm.*) Smell.

SECRETARY (*smells*): Old Sobaco, my favorite!

SANCHO (*Snap.* MEXICAN-AMERICAN *lowers arm*): And above all, he is charming. Would you like to meet him?

SECRETARY: Oh yes!

SANCHO (*Snap.* MEX-AM *turns toward* SANCHO): Eric?

(*To* SECRETARY): We call him Eric Garcia.

(*To* ERIC): I want you to meet Miss JIM-enez, Eric.

MEXICAN-AMERICAN: Miss JIM-enez, I am delighted to make your acquaintance. (*He kisses her hand.*)

SECRETARY: Oh, my, how charming!

SANCHO: Don't say I didn't warn you.

SECRETARY: How about boards, does he function on boards?

SANCHO: You name them, he is on them. Parole boards, draft boards, school boards, taco quality control boards, surf boards, two-by-fours.

SECRETARY: Does he function in politics?

SANCHO: Señorita, you are looking at a political *machine*. Have you ever heard of the OEO, ECC, COD, War on Poverty? That's our model! Not only that, he makes political speeches.

SECRETARY: May I hear one?

SANCHO: With pleasure. (*Snap.*) Eric, give us a speech.

MEXICAN-AMERICAN: Mr. Congressman, Mr. Chairman, members of the board, honored guests, ladies and gentlemen. (SANCHO *and* SECRETARY *applaud.*) Please, please. I come before you as a Mexican-American to tell you about the problems of the Mexican. The problems of the Mexican stem from one thing and one thing alone: He's stupid. He's uneducated. He needs to stay in school. He needs to be ambitious, forward-looking, harder-working. He needs to think American, American, American, AMERICAN, AMERICAN, AMERICAN, AMERICAN, GOD BLESS AMERICA! GOD BLESS AMERICA! GOD BLESS AMERICA!! (*He goes out of control.*)

(SANCHO *snaps frantically and the* MEXICAN-AMERICAN *finally slumps forward, bending at the waist.*)

SECRETARY: Oh my, he's patriotic too!

SANCHO: Sí, señorita, he loves his country. Let me just make a little adjustment here. (*Stands* MEXICAN-AMERICAN *up.*)

SECRETARY: What about upkeep? Is he economical?

SANCHO: Well, no. I won't lie to you, the Mexican-American costs a little bit more, but you get what you pay for. He is worth every extra cent. You can keep him running on dry martinis, Langendorf bread.

SECRETARY: Apple pie?

SANCHO: Only mom's. Of course, he's also programmed to eat Mexican food on ceremonial functions, but I must warn you: An overdose of beans will plug up his exhaust.

SECRETARY: Fine! There's just one more question: *How much do you want for him?*

SANCHO: Well, I tell you what I'm gonna do. Today and today, only, because you've been so sweet, I'm gonna let you steal this model from me! I'm gonna let you drive him off the lot for the simple price of . . . let's see, taxes and license included . . . fifteen thousand dollars.

SECRETARY: Fifteen thousand *dollars?* For a *Mexican!*

SANCHO: Mexican? What are you talking, lady? This is a Mexican-*American!* We had to melt down two Pachucos, a farmworker, and a revolucionario to make this model! You want quality, you gotta pay for it! This is no cheap runabout. He's got class!

SECRETARY: Okay, I'll take him.

SANCHO: You will?

SECRETARY: Here's your money.

SANCHO: You mind if I count it?

SECRETARY: Go right ahead.

SANCHO: Oh, do you want me to wrap him up for you? We have a box in the back.

SECRETARY: No thank you. The governor is having a luncheon this afternoon, and we need a brown face in the crowd. How do I drive him?

SANCHO: Just snap your fingers. He'll do anything you want.

(SECRETARY *snaps.* MEXICAN-AMERICAN *steps forward.*)

MEXICAN-AMERICAN: RAZA QUERIDA, VAMOS LEVANTANDO ARMAS PARA LIBERARNOS DE ESTOS DESGRACIADOS GA-BACHOS QUE NOS EXPLOTAN! VAMOS . . .

SECRETARY: What did he say?

SANCHO: Something about lifting arms, killing white people, etc.

SECRETARY: But he's not supposed to say that!

SANCHO: Look, lady, don't blame me for bugs from the factory. He's your Mexican-American, you bought him, now drive him off the lot!

SECRETARY: But he's broken!

SANCHO: Try snapping another finger.

(SECRETARY *snaps.* MEXICAN-AMERICAN *comes to life again.*)

MEXICAN-AMERICAN: ESTA GRAN HUMANIDAD HA DICHO BASTA! Y SE HA PUESTO EN MARCHA! BASTA! BASTA! VIVA LA RAZA! VIVA LA CAUSA! VIVA LA HUELGA! VIVAN LOS BROWN BERETS! VIVA LOS ESTUDIANTES! CHICANO POWER!

(*The* MEXICAN-AMERICAN *turns toward the* SECRETARY, *who gasps and backs up. He keeps turning toward* JOHNNY PACHUCO, *the* FARM-WORKER, *and the* REVOLUCIONARIO, *snapping his fingers and turning each of them on, one by one.*)

JOHNNY PACHUCO (*Snap. To* SECRETARY): I'm going to get you, baby! VIVA LA RAZA!

FARMWORKER (*Snap. To* SECRETARY): Viva la Huelga! VIVA LA HUELGA!

REVOLUCIONARIO (*Snap. To* SECRETARY): Viva la Revolución! VIVA LA REVOLUCIÓN!

(JOHNNY PACHUCO, *the* FARMWORKER, *and the* REVOLUCIONARIO *join together and advance toward the* SECRETARY, *who backs up and runs out of the shop, screaming.* SANCHO *is at the other end of the shop holding his money in his hand. All freeze. After a few seconds of silence,* JOHNNY PACHUCO *moves and stretches, shaking his arms and loosening up. The* FARMWORKER *and the* REVOLUCIONARIO *do the same.* SANCHO *stays where he is, frozen to his spot.*)

JOHNNY PACHUCO: Man, that was a long one, ese. (*Others agree with him.*)

FARMWORKER: How did we do?

JOHNNY PACHUCO: Perty good, look all that lana, man. (*He goes over to* SANCHO *and removes the money from his hand.* SANCHO *stays where he is.*)

REVOLUCIONARIO: En la madre, look at all the money.

JOHNNY PACHUCO: We keep this up, we're going to be rich.

FARMWORKER: They think we're machines.

REVOLUCIONARIO: Burros.

JOHNNY PACHUCO: Puppets.

MEXICAN-AMERICAN: The only thing I don't like is . . . how come I always get to play the goddamn Mexican-American?

JOHNNY PACHUCO: That's what you get for finishing high school.

FARMWORKER: How about our wages, ese?

JOHNNY PACHUCO: Here it comes right now. Three thousand for you, three thousand for you, three thousand for you, and three thousand for me. The rest we put back into the business.

MEXICAN-AMERICAN: Too much, man. Heh, where you vatos going tonight?

FARMWORKER: I'm going over to Concha's. There's a party.

JOHNNY PACHUCO: Wait a minute, vatos. What about our salesman? I think he needs an oil job.

REVOLUCIONARIO: Leave him to me.

(JOHNNY PACHUCO, *the* FARMWORKER, *and the* MEXICAN-AMERICAN *exit, talking loudly about their plans for the night. The* REVOLU-CIONARIO *goes over to* SANCHO, *removes his derby hat and cigar, lifts him up, and throws him over his shoulder.* SANCHO *hangs loose, lifeless.*)

REVOLUCIONARIO (*to the* AUDIENCE): He's the best model we got. Ajua!

(*Exit.*)

NOTES ON CHICANO THEATER

What is Chicano theater? It is theater as beautiful, rasquachi, human, cosmic, broad, deep, tragic, comic, as the life of the Raza itself. At its high point Chicano theater is religion—the huelguistas de Delano praying at the shrine of the Virgin de Guadelupe, located in the rear of an old station wagon parked across the road from Di-Giorgio's camp No. 4; at its low point, it is a cuento or a chiste told somewhere in the recesses of the barrio, puro pedo.

Chicano theater then is first a reaffirmation of *life*. That is what all theater is supposed to do, of course; but the limp, superficial, gringo seco productions in the "professional" American theater (and the college and university drama departments that serve it) are so antiseptic, they are anti-biotic (anti-life). The characters and life situations emerging from our little teatros are too real, too full of sudor, sangre, and body smells to be boxed in. Audience participation is no cute trick with us; it is a pre-established, pre-assumed privilege. "Qué le suenen la campanita!"

Defining Chicano theater is a little like defining a Chicano car. We can start with a low-rider's cool Merc, or a campesino's banged-up Chevy, and describe the various paint jobs, hub caps, dents, taped windows, Virgin on the dashboard, etc., that define the car as particularly Raza. Underneath all the trimmings, however, is an unmistakable Detroit production, an extension of General Motors. Consider now a theater that uses the basic form, the vehicle, created by Broadway or Hollywood: that is, the "realistic" play. Actually, this type of play was created in Europe, but where French, German, and Scandinavian playwrights went beyond realism and naturalism long ago, commercial gabacho theater refuses to let go.

It reflects a characteristic "American" hangup on the material aspect of human existence. European theater, by contrast, has been influenced since around 1900 by the unrealistic, formal rituals of Oriental theater.

What do Oriental and European theater have to do with teatros Chicanos? Nothing, except we are talking about a theater that is particularly our own, not another imitation of the gabacho. If we consider our origins, say the theater of the Mayans or the Aztecs, we are talking about something totally unlike the realistic play, and something more Chinese or Japanese in spirit. Kabuki, as a matter of fact, started some time ago as something like our actos and evolved over the centuries into the highly exciting art form it is to-day; but it still contains pleberias. It evolved from and still belongs to el pueblo japonés.

In Mexico, before the coming of the white man, the greatest examples of total theater were, of course, the human sacrifices. *El Rabinal Achi,* one of the few surviving pieces of indigenous theater, describes the sacrifice of a courageous guerrillero who, rather than dying passively on the block, is granted the right to fight until he is killed. It is a tragedy, naturally, but it is all the more transcendent because of the guerrillero's identification, through sacrifice, with God. The only "set" such a drama-ritual needed was a stone block. Nature took care of the rest.

But since the Conquest, Mexico's theater, like its society, has had to imitate Europe and, in recent times, the United States. In this same vein, Chicanos in Spanish classes are frequently involved in productions of plays by Lope de Vega, Calderón de la Barca, Tirso de Molina, and other classic playwrights. Nothing is wrong with this, but it does obscure the Indio fountains of Chicano culture. Is Chicano theater, in turn, to be nothing but an imitation of gabacho playwrights, with barrio productions of racist works by Eugene O'Neill and Tennessee Williams? Will Broadway produce a Chicano version of *Hello Dolly* now that it has produced a black one?

The nature of Chicanismo calls for a revolutionary turn in the arts as well as in society. Chicano theater must be revolutionary in technique as well as content. It must be popular, subject to no other critics except the pueblo itself; but it must also educate the pueblo toward an appreciation of *social change,* on and off the stage.

It is particularly important for teatro Chicano to draw a distinction between what is theater and what is reality. A demonstration with a thousand Chicanos, all carrying flags and picket signs, shouting CHICANO POWER! is not the revolution. It is theater about the revolution. The people must act in *reality,* not on stage (which could be anywhere, even on a sidewalk) in order to achieve real change. The Raza gets excited, but unless the demonstration evolves into a street battle (which has not happened yet but is possible), it is basically a lot of emotion with very little political power, as Chicanos have discovered by picketing, demonstrating, and shouting before school boards, police departments, and stores to no avail.

Such guerrilla theater passing as a demonstration has its uses, of course. It is agitprop theater, as the gabachos used to call it in the thirties: agitation and propaganda. It helps stimulate and sustain the mass strength of a crowd. Hitler was very effective with this kind of theater, from the swastika (卐) to the Wagneresque stadium at Nuremburg. On the other end of the political spectrum, the huelga march to Sacramento in 1966 was pure guerrilla theater. The red-and-black thunderbird flags of the UFWOC (then NFWA) and the standards of the Virgen de Guadelupe challenged the bleak sterility of Highway 99. Its emotional impact was irrefutable. Its actual political impact was somewhat less. Governor Brown was not at the state Capitol, and only one grower, Schenley Industries, signed a contract. Later contracts have been won through a brilliant balance between highly publicized events that gained public support (marches, Cesar's fast, visits by Reuther, Robert and Ted Kennedy, etc.) and actual hard-ass door-to-door, worker-to-worker, organizing. Like Delano, other aspects of the Chicano movement must remember what is teatro and what is reality.

But beyond the mass struggle of La Raza in the fields and barrios of America, there is an internal struggle in the very corazón of our people. That struggle, too, calls for revolutionary change. Our belief in God, the Church, the social role of women—these must be subject to examination and redefinition on some kind of public forum. And that again means teatro. Not a teatro composed of actos or agitprop but a teatro of ritual, of music, of beauty, and of spiritual sensitivity. A teatro of legends and myths. A teatro of religious strength. This type of theater will require real dedication; it may, indeed, require a couple of generations of Chicanos devoted to the use of the theater as an instrument in the evolution of our people.

The teatros in existence today reflect the most intimate understanding of everyday events in the barrios from which they have emerged. But, if Aztlan is to become reality, then we as Chicanos must not be reluctant to act nationally—to think in national terms, politically, economically, spiritually. We must destroy the deadly regionalism that keeps us apart. The concept of a national theater for La Raza is intimately related to our evolving nationalism in Aztlan.

Consider a Teatro Nacional de Aztlan that performs with the same skill and prestige as the Ballet Folklórico de México (not for gabachos, however, but for the Raza). Such a teatro could carry the message of La Raza into Latin America, Europe, Japan, Africa—in short, all over the world. It would draw its strength from all the small teatros in the barrios, in terms of people and their plays, songs, designs; and it would give back funds, training, and augmenting strength of national unity. One season the teatro members would be on tour with the Teatro Nacional; the next season they would be back in the barrio sharing their skills and experience. It would accommodate about 150 people altogether, with 20 to 25 in the Nacional and the rest spread out in various parts of Aztlan, working with the campesino, the urbano, the mestizo, the piojo, etc.

Above all, the national organization of teatros would be self-supporting and independent, meaning no government grants. The corazón de la Raza cannot be revolutionized on a grant from Uncle Sam. Though many of the teatros, including El Campesino, have been born out of pre-established political groups—thus making them harbingers of that particular group's viewpoint, news, and political prejudices—there is yet a need for independence for the following reasons: objectivity, artistic competence, survival. El Teatro Campesino was born in the huelga, but the very huelga would have killed it if we had not moved sixty miles to the north of Delano. A struggle like the huelga needs every person it can get to serve its immediate goals in order to survive; the Teatro, as well as the clinic, service center, and newspaper being less important at the moment than the survival of the union, were always losing people to the grape boycott. When it became clear to us that the UFWOC would succeed and continue to grow, we felt it was time for us to move and begin speaking about things beyond the huelga: Vietnam, the barrio, racial discrimination, etc.

The teatros must never get away from the Raza. Without the palomia sitting there, laughing, crying, and sharing whatever is onstage, the teatros will dry up and die. If the Raza will not come to theater, then the theater must go to the Raza. This, in the long run, will determine the shape, style, content, spirit, and form of el teatro Chicano.

Pachucos, campesinos, low-riders, pintos, chavalonas, familias, cuñados, tíos, primos, Mexican-Americans, all the human essence of the barrio is starting to appear in the mirror of our theater. With them come the joys, sufferings, disappointments, and aspirations of our gente. We challenge Chicanos to become involved in the art, the lifestyle, the political and religious act of doing teatro.

Dear Nancy

The main street (there's really no other) in San Juan Bautista is called (obviously) Main Street. The feel of the town is Monterrey-Mexican: lots of Spanish-flavored architecture, two or three Mexican restaurants, an old mission, and a gaggle of antique stores. There is one "fine" restaurant, The Brass Lantern, filled with middle-aged couples; the men wear turtleneck sweaters, the ladies shirtwaist dresses.

It's seven in the evening now, and San Juan Bautista at seven in the evening is almost dead. The gas station's resident high school mechanic and gas jockey is smiling coyly at two girls with hair curlers who have parked demurely across the street in a 1961 two-tone Chevy. The antique stores, leather boutique, and the Mission Cafe are all closed.

San Juan Bautista has basically only one good street aside from Main: Third Street. The paving is shot to hell on Second and Fourth, and the sidestreets are in any case dotted with houses, not business.

I got here this afternoon, coming from a Teatro performance in Santa Clara, where both companies of the Teatro celebrated the 96th anniversary of the execution of Tibuercio Vasquez with a performance at Santa Clara College, a private, Catholic school, and then a march to Vasquez' gravesite—a seven-block walk from the college.

Vasquez was, according to local lore, a bandit. But as Luis said at the graveyard, "Tibuercio Vasquez was a guerrilla, not a bandit. History has distorted his role. He took from the people who stole, and gave to those who had been stolen from.

"Tibuercio Vasquez," he continued, "is representative of our Chicano heritage, which has been buried all around us, without us knowing. It's buried, and distorted by the gabacho historians who want us to believe only their lies.

"Well, Vasquez was a hero. Remember that. And remember this day—it belongs to all Chicanos everywhere."

The march culminated the day's activities in Santa Clara. Before that there had been a performance of actos—the most powerful being *Las Calaveras de Tibuercio Vasquez,* an acto in classic style about the life and death of Vasquez. The roles in the Calaveras are all portrayed as skeletons with costumes over back leotards on which are painted bones—as a matter of fact, at one point a figure comes on stage with a birthday cake, and the assembled cast of specters sings "Happy Muerte to you, Happy Muerte to you, Happy Muerte Tibuercio Vasquez, Happy Muerte to you."

Death is an important thing in Mexican folklore—Luis first saw the skeleton costumes used by a troupe from Mexico called Los Moscarones. He's adapted the costumes for his own needs, and they're common now in a lot of the actos.

The graveside ceremony was simple and, frankly, moving. A small girl—she couldn't have been more than four—placed a bunch of flowers on Vasquez' grave, Luis said words, and people filed out. There must have been 150 or so who showed up. Luis said later that it was more than he expected.

The drive from Santa Clara was beautiful once I got off the main roads. The land around San Juan—towns like Hollister—are full of the aura that Steinbeck wrote about in *The Grapes of Wrath.* They're agricultural communities, filled with people who migrated during the Depression, and who, unfortunately, bear little affection for the Chicanos who pass through looking for work.

Example: Just after I arrived in San Juan Bautista, Danny Valdez, who heads the company there, asked if I'd like to ride into Hollister to pick up some lumber. There had been some money sent for that purpose from Fresno, and the lumber yard was right by the Western Union. We drove down in a panel truck, past incredibly green fields, through the dry but not oppressive hotness of Hollister's outskirts—bars, abandoned cars, broken picket fences—and finally got into town. Danny and I went inside the WU office to pick up the cash. The clerk was most harsh in his manner, keeping Danny waiting, demanding all sorts of identification, and finally, when he handed the money over with all of the grace Ole Captain Cotchipee might have had if he handed the deed for Big Bethel to Purlie Victorious, he looked at Danny and said, "Don't get drunk, boy, y'heah? You stay sober now."

And when we went to the lumber yard, we waited until I finally couldn't take it any longer, and asked in my best New York accent when the hell we were getting served.

At any rate, we finally got the lumber back to the theater, a two-story white wood building with a large backyard, an interior court, and an attached (but as yet unopened) restaurant. The inside of the theater is painted beautifully and simply—the roof in red-and-pink stripes, the woodwork natural, and the trim on the walls, yellow. The stage is shallow—ten feet deep and maybe seventeen wide, with two permanent sets of black drapes hung from the rafters.

No real theater seats yet, just sixty-four fake wrought-iron chairs—like from ice cream parlors—and focusing the lights means adjusting the coffee cans that ring the photo-floods that Danny and his crew have hung precariously.

There is a lobby, though, filled with posters, and a bar, where you can get beer and soft drinks, and room to get dressed backstage. And it is indeed a real theater. It has the feel, the smells, the gestalt of a real theater, as much as any summerstock house I've been in.

Most importantly, the theater has a Mexican feel to it. The adjoining restaurant is old—it looks like adobe—and even though this *centro cultural* is in its first weeks, the Chicanos in San Juan and the surrounding area have started coming to see the Teatro, and getting involved in its activities.

The company here is young—except for Daniel, they're all students at one or another of the colleges in the San Jose-Santa Clara area, which means they drive a sixty-five-mile round trip to work at the theater. They're kids like Sal Bravo, a student at San Jose State, who got into the Teatro because it's part of the movement.

"I never had any experience in theater," he told me. "But I play the guitar, and when I saw Danny's group—the Teatro Urbano—about a year ago, I went in thinking like a Mexican-American and came out thinking like a Chicano. I saw what La Raza could be, and I wanted to help out."

I did, too. Which meant that I painted, mopped the floor, and helped the crew put up the chairs before the evening's performance, the first official performance of the Teatro in their newest theater.

And, sitting in the back of the house during the show, with all the sixty-four seats filled, whole families sitting together, laughing at the actos, being happy and communally proud of their Chicano-ness, I really began to see what Luis and Daniel have been talking about. Sure, the skits are entertaining—and funny. But they go deep. They use what our leading Jewish writer, Elie Wiesel, calls collective memory—that is, the emotional pitch of each acto plucks a chord inside every Chicano, because he is a culmination of his entire culture and history, no matter how much he tries to fight it.

I remember a character in Joseph Wambaugh's *The New Centurions* who tries to hide his Mexican ancestry. But he likes eating Chicano food—no matter how much he gorges himself on steak and potatoes, there's a drive somewhere inside his soul that's satisfied best by frijoles and chile verde. Just like Luis and his bologna sandwiches, no?

That's what happened to the crowd at the Teatro. They just became, for an evening, intensely proud to be part of La Raza. They had, in Luis' words, found the corazón that America took away from them. And that, Nancy, made me smile.

Tomorrow we go off to Soledad. I'll let you know what happens there, as there's some question as to whether or not we'll be admitted. There were two stabbings last weekend, and the place is secured, according to the latest reports.

Be well.

Love,

j

King City, California

Dear Nancy

The access road to Soledad prison is bordered by neatly pruned shrubs and tall, impressive evergreen trees. As you turn off Highway 101, all you can see are the blocklike ochre buildings and a tall smokestack. Coming closer, down the straight, long driveway, the fences become predominant—tall industrial-quality wire constructions, topped with a triple strand of barbed wire.

The gatehouse is manned by a guard who, at a distance of three hundred feet, can speak to incoming cars through an intercom placed conveniently at the side of the road. It's like the Jack in the Box Drive-In syndrome reduced to absolute absurdity.

The gatehouse guard also has a speaker system that reaches into the visitor's waiting room. And he can listen, too, so conversation is very soft there.

I got to the prison just before the Teatro showed up, so that I could get some rest—I have to drive to Los Angeles tonight, and be at the Bodacious Buggerrilla, a black street theater, tomorrow morning. The Teatro was invited to Soledad by GEMA, the prison's Chicano organization, to perform in the library—right inside the lockup. What a first—a revolutionary theater performing inside a prison.

Danny Valdez was excited. "This is what it's really all about," he told me. "We're going to give the vatos inside a taste of what the real world's all about. No bullshit, no half-ass song and dance about how great it is to be Mexican. I want to tell it like it is—this is a real people's theater, and tonight it's really being taken to the people.

"And I'm proud to see that at Soledad—a Spanish name, right? —that the Chicanos are getting it together. They have a real stake in this state—in this country.

"We're a hybrid people now, Chicanos are. We were raped by the Spaniards, and then by the Americanos. Hence the Teatro, which is trying to show people there's more to the Chicano image than the Frito Bandito. And I think that the prisoners here can really identify with us—because we'll show them that cats like Joaquin and Tibuercio Vasquez weren't ignorant horse-thieves, but real guerrilleros, who stated publicly again and again that they were fighting against the rape of their people by the white society.

"So while we're not here to cast a false image on what being a Chicano is in the outside world, we do want to tell the pintos at Soledad that brown is good—and to be proud of their heritage. And we're also here to show them that their brothers on the outside are thinking of them, too."

The core of Soledad is a concrete corridor perhaps forty feet wide and more than a quarter-mile long. It's secured at each end, and in the middle, by massive electronically controlled iron-bar doors (Adam Locking Device: Folger Adam Prison cell constructor/ Penal engineering/Joliet, Illinois). From the core hallway you can get into any of the cellblocks in the facility.

What a sight, as we came through the doors, playing guitars, pretty Chicanas in miniskirts, tee-shirted guys with a box of props, and lots of singing and noise. The prisoners—and the guards—were astonished.

When things got set up in the library, I got a chance to talk with some of the prisoners. Most of them are in on robbery or assault, and the guys that I talked with consider themselves political prisoners. They said that even though Jerry Enomoto, the deputy warden, is a third-world cat, he's still holding down the size of ethnic organizations inside the place. And one said, frankly, that he was amazed that Enomoto allowed the Teatro inside Soledad at all.

There was only one guard on duty inside the library when the actos started, and I asked a prisoner why. He walked me over to the window, where I could see a gunrail, and six screws with weapons. The one guard (an older, Chicano guy) is a sacrificial lamb if anything goes wrong, he told me.

Over a cup of tepid, weak Soledad coffee I asked a couple of the guys from GEMA how they felt about the Teatro—aside from the obvious fact that they were overjoyed to have some Chicano entertainment. The gist of what they said was that the Teatro is exactly what the Chicano prisoners at Soledad need—a group of people to raise their consciousness; to make them realize that being brown ain't that bad.

"This prison is a fuckin' nuthouse," said one guy. "Really, it's gonna explode soon, if something isn't done. There's no rehabilitation. The parole board is a joke—ten minutes a year with them, if you're lucky—and the dehumanizing process that goes on inside is completely unbelievable. So what's left? Books, when they're not censored, our newspaper, which is really a PR rag for the prison, and our entertainment, which is usually a drag; and GEMA, which, although it's being stifled by the warden, is still the best thing we got going. At least with an ethnic organization, you know your brothers are around to take care of you. Some people may call that racist. I don't, because my brothers are how I stay alive in this place. And if the Teatro can get inside here—which they have—and do some shows to make me happy—or proud—to be a Bronce, then that makes me a better man than I was yesterday. And maybe most important, it makes me feel like a man.

"Goddamn, you know how fuckin' good it feels to raise my fist and shout Viva La Raza!? I belong. I'm not a number any more when I do that."

That was the reaction. And at the end of the show, when the prisoners stood and cheered they shouted Viva La Raza! so loud that people walking through the hall outside the library looked in to see what was happening. Then they started to embrace the members of the Teatro, who gave back embrace for embrace. For a few minutes, the insanity of Soledad and what it stands for was forgotten. The inmates were more than numbers; they became, through theater, real people again. If I were to say they regained some lost humanity you might accuse me of pretentions, but that's exactly what happened in that locked, barred, guarded library.

We stayed in Soledad for maybe two and a half hours. It was some of the best theater I've ever seen in my life, because the audience was totally and completely involved in every single thing that went on. They sang, clapped, and shouted. They were, well, men for a while, instead of numbers—cyphers. And that showed, too, on all of us as we left. The Teatro people were happy folk as we went through the series of electronic gates that gave us freedom.

"I just would have liked to bring those cats with us," Danny said, as the gate slid shut and the circuit switched off behind us.

"Shit, I could put together a bitch of a show using them."

He's right. Very.

Love,

j

THE PURPOSE OF THE BODACIOUS BUGGERRILLA
IS TO EXPOSE THE SYSTEM'S PIE BY GATHERING
AND SPREADING INFORMATION

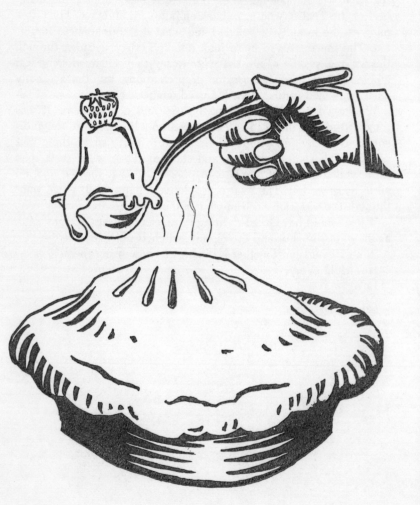

RECIPE FOR THE SYSTEM'S PIE

1/3 cup INSTITUTIONALIZATION
  (Any combination of the following ingredients)

  Religion
  Education
  Marriage
  Business
  Military
  Prisons
  Mental hospitals
  Government

1/3 cup STATUS
  (Any combination of the following ingredients)

  House on the hill
  Color television
  Yacht
  White-collar jobs
  Travel
  Bank account
  Blond hair
  Friends

1/3 cup OPPRESSION
  (Any combination of the following ingredients)

  Ghettos
  Sickness
  Hunger
  Self-hate
  Racism
  Capitalism

BRAINWASH THOROUGHLY.

PLACE IN A CRUST OF ECLECTIC PROCESS AND THINKING.

BAKE AT LOW CONSCIOUSNESS LEVEL
(CAUTION: DO NOT LET PIE REACH BOILING POINT)

WHEN DONE, TOP WITH IMITATION DEMOCRACY.

Berkeley, California

Journal: Tuesday

Got off a call today to Ed Bereal of the Bodacious Buggerrilla in Los Angeles. Finally spoke to him—a strange-sounding cat on the phone. Bereal says he'd be happy to talk to me, went on to say that he'll get off some material about what the Buggerrilla's been doing. He asked if I have a cassette machine. Otherwise an uneventful day. Unable to get over to talk to the Mime Troupe. Sit tight and wait.

Ed Bereal to John Weisman: transcript of a taped letter.

I just want to address myself to you generally, and that way I can kind of talk; I can let my head just take me where it wants to go. Not so much even address myself to anything definite or what you want to know or any of that—I guess I'm just gamin' with myself, bullshittin' with me—which I find really isn't any bullshit. Some of the shit we used to think was crazy or far out really applies right now. But just to talk or to get a good feeling out of communication sometimes says a lot more than anything else. My consciousness level is at a higher level; consciousness generally is at a higher level. Just wow, goddammit I said something really bitchin', boy; I was doin' it, you know. People find out—and that's real communication on everything—that *everything is everything*—like Mae West talking a sexual relationship with Cary Grant—I look at it now, and the United States of Amerika is indicted. You know, what you do a thing *for* doesn't mean that that's where it's comin' *from*. So that I can probably talk to you right now about my love of—I used to love airplanes and I used to love flying—I once jumped off the roof. I could maybe talk to you about that and maybe tell you much more about myself or what I'm into or how I see things than if I was to try to talk about that directly. You know, do you see what I'm sayin'? So like just to rap sometimes is what it's all about or just to write—whatever is whatever, you know, because everything is all connected up. And whenever I do anything, it's automatically in relationship; it's automatically in context. It's just "Am I hip enough? Are you hip enough?"

In just thinkin' about the Buggerrilla and lookin' back in time, it's really heavy because you can see decisions you made at a particular time and the reasons you made those decisions; and the way it turned out might not have had anything to do with what was whippin' in your head at the time. But more and more it's turnin' into what it should be. It's almost out of my hands, you know, out of control, which is to show it's very much in control; I mean it's dealin' with what should be dealt with right now. And my original concept of the whole thing was somethin' else, very romantic.

I was very knocked out about getting a group of people together because I was schooled in an art school. My real talent, I guess, if I have it . . . I was going to say my real talent lies in my hands, but my hands are just the tools; my head really does it. One of the things I always believed was that if a thing is steppin' around in your head, you'll apply it to any area. You can apply it to any area. There are some—if you are a short guy with little hands, it might be best that you write rather than play the piano 'cause your hands like can't make all them octaves. But if you decide to do it in music, then if your head is right, you'll come up with another way to play the piano, which ain't by the rules as we know 'em now. Maybe you gotta get a special piano designed with huge keys so you can only hit one note rather than any number, and yours comes out slow and really weird, you know. My point bein' that as long as your head, as long as your over-all concept [is] of some kind of an aesthetic thing (and that's how I got into my original thought of the theater, I came in purely on an aesthetic level. I had some political education; I was somehow reacting to my condition). But my real thing— and still is really, but it's different now—was to be able to get say twelve or thirteen people who were dynamite, who did dynamite, who just blew shit up cause they did it that way, you know. And people could learn or be knocked out by, wow, man, certain possibilities, you know; like a lot of possibilities that they could deal with, you know.

My initial thing in terms of guerrilla theater was the exciting, the aesthetic part of it. What I have come to find out—and I kind of knew this part of it then—is that *how* you do a thing can be as political as *what* you do. I didn't fully appreciate it like I do now, but aesthetics, just the idea of, say, for instance, the ability to go wherever your head takes you, you know, the whole creative process can really be a political thing in the sense that—one of the things that disenfranchised people, what happens to them, is they get ripped off of their imagination. They're so into like the Monday and like get that meal, man; that's all you got to think about; get that fuckin' meal, you know. And especially because in most capitalist societies, they run a whole thing that you're less than me; you're dumb; you're stupid; you can't think; you know, you take orders; and poor peoples' thing daily is takin' orders. That's why the black cats come home and shoot their wives; "that's a bunch of shit; 'I want you to DO.' Hey, I had to DO all day; you know, don't run this on me." So what happens is like it gets ripped off from you, man. The whole 'what if' concept. Like what if I decided to tie a ribbon on my joint, you know; I mean a Nixon ribbon, man. With a picture of him on it, right; 'cause I think that's just gonna win the people if I . . . I mean, like nobody ever trips or is able to do that because that's expensive; that's a luxury, man; and poor, disenfranchised people don't have no luxuries at all. You know, they balls to the wall.

So that what happens is that I've come to know—and I knew partially then, but I know more just out and out straight political level than I did then—that the way you do a thing, the ability, is important. I think the people can pick up how your head goes by lookin' at your thing, whatever it is. I mean if it's really far out, I mean if you're usin' means—I'm not talkin' about content; I'm talkin' about packaging—if you're usin' means that are creative for the first time, man, like it really makes people see. I think that can inspire them. I think that can go—like when we do *Uncle Tom,* you know, I mean they go No Shit; Yeah! Hey, I understand that; hey, that is An Idea. And they'll deal.

In any case, what happened was like I just picked up on the thrill of the visual nut 'cause it cooked up with my whole art background and like where paintings are and I'm visually oriented very much anyway personally. And on a group level, I'm verbally oriented 'cause that's my cultural kind of thing, you know, you rap. So that like when I'm first doing the group, tryin' to get the group together, it was primarily because of the image of a group of people doing some really far-out shit on a street corner someplace or snatchin' people or pullin' a thing, just a very far-out thing. Everybody's all up and excited and shit, and you go oh no no no we just playin'; you know, we just playin'; no really, it wasn't real. 'Course, if any of this makes any difference, you know, maybe you oughta take it; it's yours; give it away, you know. That kind of romance; it's a little bit romantic in that way.

What's happened now is that the group is organized on another level, and it's really taken my original idea and gone like where it should go with it. I think again another thing is that if you offer a creative thing—no, let me put it this way—a creative thing with one cat is one thing; a creative thing with 12 people being very creative and coming off of each other is another, man. The one cat, like me a member of a group, can do heavier shit if I've got a group to run my shit on and then come back and write it down or whatever than if I'm out there cuttin' off my ear on top of a hill someplace tryin' to say, you know, whatever you say on top of a hill after you cut off your ear. That collective situation, I've really learned the value of it. I tend to be a loner, and I still maintain that partly; but I do need the collective; I really do need it. And because it's a collective, much more can get done. And the group for one reason or another really mirrors certain things I think about. And it's just as if—I think every member of the group can feel it—it's just as if each member of the group—say that you're talkin' about 10 people, somebody just got 18 more arms. I mean, I just got 18 more arms, 18 more legs, 9 more heads, man, and it's like having a computer with me: all kinda other things go down.

So all that, man, is on one level, you know, on how do you move and how do you deal. At the same time, on another level, is, okay, now can you bring this collective together, like an arrow, and hit that spot, that creative spot? Can you hit some invisible point, bringing it together, man, because making 12 people work as one is really a heavy tune. I mean, it's a contradiction; you really dig individuality or the creativeness of an individual there as you sit in the circle and make whatever decision you wanna make. But at the same time, once certain decisions have been made and plans of action have been chosen, then it's all got to come together. And it moves like a well-coordinated centipede. It's got a whole bunch of things goin' but the body is destined for that point. And yet that point is often individually arrived at.

It's like a book I read once, like there was a group of kids, and each kid had a specific thing that he did. There was a little baby involved. (It was science fiction.) The little baby was a computer who could compute. But it took another child, who was a deci-pherer, to read from the computer and give it out for the director, who was the guy who could take the information and point it in the direction, you know. And there was two other kids who could levitate who got it done, you know. But at any one point, it was in somebody's hands and at that point he was the leader. What's heavy is to be able to chart where a group goes; and say okay, there's gotta be one guy who goes there. One guy says okay, we do it this way. Another guy says I'm the one that does it; and another guy says this is where you gotta do it. And everybody, the whole group, says okay, we point that way. And then all the parts come in and some-body else says hold it, man, we're not efficient enough; we're not snappy enough; hey, you've gotta start doin' this. And it all moves in and out from this head into another head; and by the time the end result happens, it's a muther fucker. But it's still a balance be-tween a group of people and like one guy callin' the shots.

All that is kind of like a lot of theory shit. The real number when it gets down to it is talkin' to the people, man; and try to get this muthafucker straight—the United States of Amerika—which is a trip. We can theorize for days, but it's gotta get down to Does It Work? Can You Change The Shit? 'Cause it's some pretty painful shit, man. Amerika is a *painful* muthafucker; I mean, it is *painful*. One of the things we were talkin' about the other day is the fact that livin' in the ghetto you gotta get used to seein' casualties, man. It's like Vietnam but on a color TV level. I mean, you know, you get a chance to watch color TV and sit there like a muthafucker. I can sit here, not only that I could wear a beautiful suit, a new suit; I could have a Cadillac car and twenty-eight, as they say on the streets, twenty-eight bitches wrapped around my arm and be in pain, I mean In Trouble, 'cause Amerika don't give a shit. You know, Amerika will fuck with you; if you gonna be here, that's your ass. You are gonna give up some ass; you are gonna give up some ass 'cause this is a bad muthafucker, man.

What happens is, what I'm tryin' to say is, you can theorize for days but regardless of what you do, you've gotta deal with this son-of-a-bitch whether you know it or not. Now, you can be unconscious and be the problem, or you can have your head together and know this shit and deal with it. And that's what the Buggerrilla obviously, ultimately, has gotta do. It's gotta come off dealing with Amerika if it don't do nothin' else on the stage. Hopefully, like I said, my romantic part of it was like how you get up there and do it. That is important, and it can deal with the situation. There are radical things that happen in technique. But at the same time, ultimately we gotta come off, the Buggerrilla's got to happen on the streets, and it's got to turn around the people on the streets. You gotta know where they're comin' from; you've got to deal with the fuckin' problems here as they are. And as you deal with it, they know, man; they know when you're dealin' and when you're bullshittin'. The people have cut loose so many guys, man, who say on a racial level, we've given up people to the mainstream of shit, man, and before you know it they're doin' Jewish folk songs, man, ain't got nothin' to do with us; and that ain't what got 'em where they got. That ain't what did it at all. What happens is like you got to stay close to the people and you gotta point your shit to that. Like, I'm not sure I know how to do, say, the cultural habits of white Appalachia, man, or of L.A., for that matter. Like I don't know how to address myself to that situation; but as far as lookin' around, the left should have been dealin' with them cats, man, 'cause that's where it is, man. All we can do, I mean, the Buggerrilla is a black group; and we can deal with black people's things. We try to deal with shit on a class level. If I knew how to appeal to them cats in the valley, I would. If I knew that shit, I would, 'cause they're in trouble, man. The point bein' that there should be a Buggerrilla out *there* that deals with *their* problems and starts to shine the light toward a whole class struggle thing. You know, it's very important.

But in any case, what I'm tryin' to say, is—and there I'm theorizin' again—you gotta hit a cat in the gut. If you don't hit a cat in the gut, you'll never find his head, never find his head. So that's kind of ultimately where we come from. We try to number one be strong and powerful on a technical level and be strong and powerful as far as where we come from ideologically. And do we talk to your hassles? Do we give you some answers? Do we ask you some pertinent questions? I mean questions that are pertinent to your situation. I'm talkin' about the wino, man; I'm talkin' about the whore; I'm talkin' about whoever is in my level of conversation; whoever I can communicate with, man; that's who I'm talkin' about. 'Cause that's where it's gotta happen. And you drop the proper information; sometimes it can be very sophisticated, very sophisticated information. You put it together right, man, they got it. If nothin' else, you gotta come off like "I Care"; you know, "I Care What's Happen'." You know, "I understand that this thing is an obscene son-of-a-bitch that we're livin' in, and here's a Band-Aid." Maybe it don't cure the disease, but like hey, you know where I'm comin' from. That's the point . . . ultimately that's where we gotta come off. And it gets stronger and stronger and stronger.

And I got this idea, a real bad thing, you know, it'd be funny to use you, man. Really, you can be like a Buggerrilla in hiding. We gotta do this show at the Ash Grove; and we were like puttin' together a piece for that. 'Cause it's hard to—like it'll probably be a predominantly white audience, and if I can't get deep off into your cultural thing and speak to that specifically—like the Rollin' Stones was always distant from me, man, but I can see that other people like young white cats, man, were findin' somethin', man, were pickin' up on somethin'. I can't supply that somethin', but I can scream about where I'm comin' from. And I'm thinkin' about this piece that might say somethin' and it just might make you flash to where you are. I mean flash to a picture that's just a little bigger than your thing.

Because as I said to you, the United States of Amerika is a muthafucker; and it is game back. I mean there are so many games, games explaining games about games in a gamin' way; man, this is insane. It's like a movie set, man; and all the front of the set, the camera side of the set is facin' white people. And they believe that all them building fronts is real. And if you go through the door, there'll be a room over them. But if you go through any one of them doors—and you better hope it's not an upstairs door—all you gonna do is run into me. I'm back there, and I know it ain't real 'cause I see the props and I know that whole thing is just about six inches thick. Sometime you'll see a porch; but don't go through that door, 'cause all you gonna see is a bunch of black people, a bunch of Chicanos; you'll even find some disenfranchised white people back there. There's a whole planet back behind that fuckin' set, man. And everybody, like senators, house of representatives, everybody—school principals and teachers—all of them, man, are doing everything on Main Street. They're tryin' to make a universe fit into one street;

like Main Street Amerika. You watch any TV show, man, it's the same shit. They're tellin' you God, country, mother—that's Main Street shit, man. Don't none of that go down, 'cause go through any one of them doors on Main Street, any one of them doors, and you're in trouble, man; you in trouble. You got to re-do your whole thing. I've often thought these cats like Richard Speck or these guys who take a rifle, got up in a tower, and blast people, you know, I have a feeling that maybe that dude found out something; man, he found out something. Like he found out this thing isn't real; he found out this is a great TV studio in the sky, Man, I don't know. 'Cause it's not real. And what happens is Nixon and whoever else, J. Edgar Hoover, all them dudes are tryin' to keep everybody on Main Street; and play like all this is the way it is; and Walt Disney made the set.

I mean, hey look at this year's Cadillac, man, just the way it looks, man; that's fuckin' chrome and glass and shit; there ain't shit behind that thing, man. There ain't nothin' behind it. First of all, it's a bad design, but there's nothin' goin' on there, man; in a year, it's dead. It's dead, man. What happens is it's all like that. I mean we're so beautifully—I gotta go back to it everything is everything, man. I got a feeling that the thing that should be written on the Amerikan flag is THE BIGGER THE BETTER. Like that's what every-body's for, and in a year it's gonna be dead 'cause there's gonna be another game. It's like the golden carrot, man; and you run up and down Main Street, man, and you never look in no windows, man; you never ask no questions. We supply all your needs, man. Okay, what the Buggerrilla's gotta do is jump through one of them fuckin' windows. Do you understand the kind of analogy I'm goin' with, man? We're backed in; we can see it's bullshit. I think every once in a while they'll let a black person on Main Street just because . . . at least according to 1930 films, there was no black people anyplace, ever. And if there were, they were of a particular kind; again, Main Street shit, that whole game to fuck up your mind. Like a black man is a pop-eyed, jumpin' up and down, silly, no-thinkin' dude; and a black woman—no black woman weighed under 350 pounds; none of 'em, man. And everybody looked at it, and they looked at the reality on the streets; and never questioned shit. No one ever ques-tions anything. So I think maybe in essence the Buggerrilla is sayin' hey, check out the shit. The beauty contest ain't even the same; it ain't the same. Think what would happen in reality, man? I'm reality, and I'm gonna leap all over you. Check me out, 'cause you gonna have to check yourself out. You are in trouble. You are in trouble.

Hey, man, let's take your field of reference, just your field of reference. If there's a whole bunch of Chinese dudes runnin' down Main Street, and you got to jump in a room, and you got to get off the street. Everybody off the streets, like Uncle Sam's shit ran thin. Everybody off the streets, you gonna jump through one of them windows; and like I said, I'm just gonna be back there with a whole bunch of Chicano and Indian and Chinese dudes. So that's what is happening, I think, with the Buggerrilla, what the Buggerrilla is committed to, is rip down fuckin' Main Street, man. Rip that son-of-a-bitch down. So when we do this play, man, we gonna let you play this thing like it's real. First, we won't even play it right the first time, but we'll play it real the first time. So that I think, like I said, we gotta jam people. There's black people behind the scenes on Main Street, livin' Main Street in their minds. And that's the Buggerrilla's job; clean your head up, man; eradicate Uncle Sam. The secret of Amerika is fuck everybody. It's like standing in a cesspool tryin' to use the water to clean yourself off. So the Buggerrilla's involved in, like not only shocking people to where shit's at; and for that you gotta do political education, you gotta stay in your own head; you gotta ask a lot of questions; you gotta come up with some kind of reality for an insane asylum. The system's dead; it's been dead; it's like givin' mouth-to-mouth resuscitation to a corpse, you know, to go along with half the shit out there. So that what we do and what we try to do is go BOO; not only am I real, but BOO, this is real; what I'm talkin' about is real. You know, come out of your little number, black or white. Wherever you are, come out of there 'cause this muthafucker's got your mind.

So what I was thinkin' about doin' is this one thing. We probably have one of the women get up onstage and after the show, say, or maybe before the show, whatever, the powerhouse thing would be to do it before the show. Say okay, this is the context in which we comin' at you. You better hang on, if you a hard-case liberal, 'cause we comin' at you really heavy. But she'd get up [after the play] and she'd say you know, "thank you very much. We're happy to be here tonight, and just to give you an idea of where we're coming from—like Watts, and maybe this is the first time we've ever been outside the ghetto. And we kind of wanted to let the people know where we're comin' from." Then say a little bit about it. "We're a street theater group, and we try to take black lives and sum it up in a little ball and run it back to you, and maybe critique that or offer up some alternatives to what's happenin'. And we are really involved socially and politically and there are some very particular things we feel about what's going on and we want to share it with you. And we really enjoy doing work for you. And we would like to talk to you after the show. I think maybe we'll even give out some questionnaires; we've been talkin' about doin' that. And just get ideas from you and maybe just an informational organ and ideas that happen in the Ash Grove, we can take back to the ghetto and give to whoever can use them." And then she'd go on maybe with "a lot of people don't like the kind of thing we do. But in spite of that, we're gonna do it anyway because we feel like people gotta have alternative information," and she'd go on and say, "because some people don't like what we do, we've gotten a few nasty notes. And even a few threats. And the other night our director got a threat that was really kind of serious and it said that the next time we go onstage, they plan to make a real concerted effort to stop us because of whatever we plan to do."

And she talk like that. And we'd have maybe, I was thinkin', man, a black cat for it; we probably will do that between now and Ash Grove. But if you did it, it would even be a heavier level, like a white guy stands up in the middle of the audience, and says, "all right, nigger, I told you niggers that you shouldn't be, that this is a bunch of Communist, low-down, dirty shit; you're just a bunch of Communists drilling a bunch of people's heads with a bunch of perverted ideas. And it's enough that you put on all that animalistic kind of stuff on the stage but to come on the way you're coming on and the whole thing, I mean I've just had about enough of this." I guess it would have to come at the end of thing. But you can really come on really crazy, and she would try to say hey, you know, be cool; and some people would say sit down. But you would get really crazy, and like when little kids fight, you'd just get yo'self all whooped up into a frenzy and reach into your pocket, pull out a gun, and fire on her, fake, you know. And really make her do a hell of a fall, blood spurting all over every place; and everybody, revolutionaries, pseudorevolutionaries would be under their girlfriends' seats. And the girlfriends just standin' and yellin' and wonderin' what happened. And then when it kind of calmed down, the girl could stand up and do a whole number, you know: "Welcome to the United States of Amerika," man. This is where this shit goes down. On one level or another, and maybe we could even go on and show them what the various kinds of levels are. 'Cause murder ain't always like that, you know, the way the system works, murder goes down very slow. Sometimes it takes thirty years of your life. The first part of the murder happens in the first ten because the first thing this country gets is your mind. But I think that might be strong enough to make 'em really go WOW. There's somethin' about guns. I think guns are a religious fetish. There's somethin' about when guns are brought out, shot, or pointed, people listen. People listen, and that's what this is about. Checkin' it out; checkin' out where they are; checkin' yourself out.

Los Angeles

Dear Nancy

I met Ed Bereal for the first time today. We've been communicating for a while—letters, like the tape one I've transcribed, and phone calls. But I never met the man before.

He's a tall cat. Dark, with this unbelievable Fu Manchu mustache that stretches down his chin on both sides. Short Afro, black tee-shirt, black jeans. Tennies. Lives on Washington Boulevard, in a storefront apartment filled with goodies—a pool table and one of the most incredible motorcycles I've ever seen. If he dressed in red, white, and blue, he'd be a black Captain Amerika on that chopper.

We sat around the chopping block that serves as his dining table and we talked—about theater, about America, about us. It was an interesting—enlightening confrontation, because Bereal is a real ideological kind of guy. He's into community organization, and highly mobile theater.

The Buggerrilla is really more than theater: It's an organization. Bereal has taken the standard operating procedures that corporations use—everything from charting the chain of command to the theater's communal responsibilities, and put them on paper. It's a hell of a thing to see. What's most rewarding is that the thing—from the short time I've been here—seems to be working.

An interesting sidelight: Hanging from the ceiling just over the choppingblock table is a microphone. Bereal tapes all the conversations that he has, and plays them back later. Interesting.

Tonight the Buggerrilla played a date in Watts. And seeing them at work was something splendid. The group—which numbers twelve—set up at one end of a black-painted hall on Western Avenue and about Forty-sixth Street. The lights were floodlights—garden variety. The crowd mostly young and militant blacks. In the outside room there were posters of Che and Malcolm X and Bobby Seale and Eldridge Cleaver and Angela Davis.

The thing that struck me about the crowd was that everyone seemed to have a close friend or relative in prison. That's what the conversations leaned toward. And more, there were prison papers from as far away as Soledad to be bought and read. Papers from four, five, six institutions.

What the Buggerrilla does is almost like an incredibly cynical minstrel show. The "Mr. Bones," though is Uncle Sam—Bereal, dressed in a toga and flag and red, white, and blue cape and hat. And Uncle Sam runs all his tricks on the foul, smelly niggers, as he refers to them. The reaction is astounding. And it's very effective theater, too—simple stuff that concentrates on running down the games that white society—or more correctly, American society, plays on black folks. Whatever, there were some loud choruses of "Right on!" after each piece.

Before I close, you should know that the Buggerrilla will have, as of tomorrow, a token honky. As Bereal mentioned in his letter, they're doing a show later this week at the Ash Grove, one of L.A.'s music clubs, called *Threat to the Buggerrilla*. I sit with the folks in the audience until the end of the show, then get up, make a ruckus, and shoot somebody on stage. Sounds like fun, no? We go into rehearsal tomorrow so we can open at the Ash Grove on Tuesday. It'll be my first time onstage in anything but a spear-carrying role in legitimate theater, and the thought of doing something that'll actually provoke some people—maybe even change their way of thinking—is exciting.

Note: We pooled our cash after the show tonight and bought some vodka and juice, and some wine. Ed has taken to smashing me on the arm and calling me a bad muthafucker of a nigger. I'm beginning to like it. More, though, I'm beginning to like the theater that he's doing.

When we run through the skit, I'll let you know what it is and how it all goes together.

Love,

j

P.S. I'm enclosing a script—called *Uncle Tom*. The Buggerrilla uses it as a curtain-raiser, and I think it's a jim-dandy play. It's also representative of the Buggerrilla's skits. The heavier stuff will follow, as soon as I can convince Bereal to let me have it. But read *Uncle Tom* and enjoy. I did.

UNCLE TOM

The stage is not lit—it is in a general work light, as if the show has not begun.

UNCLE TOM *comes through the audience, with a large janitor's push-broom, sweeping and muttering to himself as he walks. He works his way to the stage, and starts to sweep it, too. Then he sees the audience, and begins to talk to them.*

UNCLE TOM: All the hollerin' and yellin' just gon' spoil everything for folks like me, who be wantin' to do the right thing.

Fo' you know it po-lice be watchin' me too, hit'n me upside my head. I don' understan' these young peoples these days, yellin' and screamin', tellin' white folks all what they gon' do to them. Great God almighty, you just cain't be doin' dat. They ain't gon' stan' fo' it.

(*He pulls out a transistor radio and starts to turn it on, scratching at his head, his ass, his crotch. All through the speech he's pulling at himself in one way or another.*)

Jumpin' up of the television sets and talkin' all this revolution-istic mess, bull-sheeet. When Maury Wills goes want to steal secon' base, he don't be hollerin' to 'em, "Hey, I'm gon' steal secon' base, so you-all better be ready."

He don' wear no signs, he don' need no sign. He jus' be stealin' secon' base.

Damn kids, talkin' machine guns and all like that. Get themselves an' everybody else kilt. But you can't tell 'em nothin', 'cause they won' listen.

Folks is gonna have to stop talkin' so much an' start listenin'. Jus' don' listen no mo'. I tells ya, it gon' spoil everything.

I is tryin' to do my job. I knows my job, and I knows my place. There don' need be no truble if you knows yo' job . . . an' yo' place. I studies de white folks, and I knows my job. Dey shows you the right things to do if you don't be hard-headed an' just listens. My daddy taught me dat. You know how to pay 'tention. He knew what he talkin' about too. Uh-huh. Yeah he did. Pay 'tention. He taught me dis ole Negro spiritual, just ta remin' me 'bout things. It go, "I hear those gentle voices callin' Ole Black Joe."

Yep, now if Joe hadn'ta been listenin', he wouldn'ta heard no gentle voices, an' that's a fac'. Think 'bout that.

Oh, goodness gracious, it be time for de game. Let's listen to what ole Maury Wills and dem Dodgers be doin' to 'em.

(TOM *tunes in the radio. A* REVOLUTIONARY BLACK MILITANT *enters through the audience. The* REVOLUTIONARY *is dressed in black leather, beret, tinted glasses, with a big Afro. He walks in a street walk, rolling his shoulders, etc.*)

REVOLUTIONARY: I'm gonna kill the first pig I see.

In this community, pigs are everywhere; they're in the cars, on the streets, they're even in the sky. You know, I walked out my house the other night, an' me an' my ole lady were laying back, and we'd just had a little taste, y'know? And we ran out, and I was runnin' out to the store to get some more, y'know? And before I got like a block away from my crib, y'know, y'know what happened? The pigs. They had me up against the wall, searchin' me and all that shit, y'know? And y'know what fo'? For a two-year-old fucked-up parkin' ticket.

They gonna tell me they pull me over 'cause I look suspicious. Now, how many niggers you know *don't* look suspicious??? Now, that's why I'm gonna kill me the next pig I see in this community. Man, I'm gonna run some red.

(*The* REVOLUTIONARY *ad-libs some more about wasting pigs.* UNCLE TOM *just shakes his head, scratches his balls some more, and leans on his broom. Through the audience comes an* ASTROLOGY FREAK. *The* FREAK *has a headband, some incredibly trendy clothes, and is carrying a book of astrology with him. He also has a bouncy walk.* UNCLE TOM *stares at the* FREAK *in utter astonishment. The* REVOLUTIONARY *ad-libs something like "aw sheeeeit" when the* FREAK *comes up on stage.*)

(*The* FREAK *bounces up onto the stage and looks the* REVOLUTIONARY *up and down. He's not paying any attention to* UNCLE TOM.)

FREAK: Ooooooooooooh.
　Ooooooooooooooooooooooh.

Ummmmmmm-huh. Hey. Wow. Um-huh.

Hey, you the real thing, ain't you. A real black revolutionary?

Y'know, it ain't often I get to see one of you guys . . . alive.

REVOLUTIONARY: Y'all don' hear what I'm sayin'. I say I'm goan' run some red roun' here. I'm goan' kill the next fuckin' pig comes into this community.

FREAK: Ummm-huh. You are a *real* revolutionary. Hey, brother, what's your sign?

Wait, don't tell me. You don't have to say nothin', *Aries.*

(*The* FREAK *looks into his astrology book.*) I know. Angela Davis, Huey P. Newton—all them cats is Aries. You is an Aries. It show all over yourself. Hey, brother, what's your birthdate so I can make an astrological chart on you?

REVOLUTIONARY: January 23.

FREAK: Hmmmm. You ain't Aries. Hmmmm. January 23—Aquarius. Lessee . . . (*He looks through his book trying to see other Aquarians.*) Richard M. Nixon. Naw, that's the wrong cat. Well, it don't matter nothin'. All you cats lay in the same cut—we the people of the third world must unite to overthrow the capitalist pigs and all that shit, right?

REVOLUTIONARY: You didn't hear what I said. I'm gonna run some red. I gotta machine gun comin'. I'm gonna kill me the next pig I see.

UNCLE TOM: What dat you say? You don' know nothin' 'bout no machine guns. You don' be knowin' nothin' about no machine anything. You gonna go get us all killed. My oh my. (*He gets nervous.*)

REVOLUTIONARY: Get away from me, you Tom muthafucker, you jive nigger.

FREAK (*to* TOM): Hey man, what's your sign?

UNCLE TOM: Signs? Signs tell you where you comin' from and where you goin' to. I ain't worried 'bout no signs. Maury Wills don't tell nobody that he gonna steal secon' base—he don' be wearin' no signs. He don' be sayin' to nobody, Hey Folks, I is gon' steal secon' base, here I comes. He jes do it, dat all. You can't have no signs. Signs is too obvious. I know dat like I know my job an' my place.

FREAK: I know what your sign is. You born under the sign of the Tom, with Rope Rising.

REVOLUTIONARY: All you niggers ain't heard what I said. I said I'm gonna kill the next pig come into this community.

(*The* REVOLUTIONARY *ad-libs about killing pigs, as two pig-faced cops come up onstage. They're wearing blue uniforms with badges, carrying nightsticks and guns, and wearing Nazi helmets with American flag decals. The first person to see them is the* FREAK. *As he's talking,* UNCLE TOM *starts to shake.*)

FREAK: Oh-oh. Lemme look up my shit for today. Lessee, Capricorn— (FREAK *uses date of performance.*) Capricorn. Beware of confrontations with powers of authority. Damn. Well, since I'm a billygoat, and billygoats always keep their four feets on the ground, I'll be off. Now. See all you cats at the Zodiac Center, y'all hear? Later.

(*The* PIGS *look at the* FREAK *go out through the audience. They grunt and oink at each other.*)

REVOLUTIONARY: You muthafuckers lost?

(*The* PIGS *look at the* REVOLUTIONARY *and grunt.*)

REVOLUTIONARY (*crossing to the* PIGS): What you doin' in this community? You don't belong here. Y'all best split. Be gone. Y'all better split, y'hear, you fascist muthafuckers.

(*The* REVOLUTIONARY *ad-libs. The* PIGS *grunt.* UNCLE TOM *cowers behind his broom, whistling "Old Black Joe" softly to himself.*)

REVOLUTIONARY: Matter of fac', I knows some people around here who is gettin' their shit together, and if you don't get the fuck outta here now, they might get it into their heads to blow y'all away.

(*The* PIGS *look nervous. They unflap their holsters and put their hands on the pistol butts.*)

That don't scare me, fuck it. Fuck you, you pig fascist muthafuckers. Y'all think that fuckin' guns will get me scared of you pigs? It don't. We out to get you, pigs. And if you think you can come into this community like you do, you gonna have to shoot me when you do.

(*The* PIGS *shoot the* REVOLUTIONARY, *emptying their guns into him. They kick the body around a bit, then, after shaking hands across the corpse, they drag the* REVOLUTIONARY *offstage. All the while,* UNCLE TOM *is trying to hide behind the broom. He is shaking so hard the broom is hitting the stage floor like a castanet. One* PIG *motions to the other, and they go upstage to where* TOM *is cowering. A* PIG *taps on the broom handle with his nightstick, twice.* UNCLE TOM *comes off of his knees.*)

UNCLE TOM: Hello? Who dat?

(*To* PIG): Howdy, boss. Um-huh, you both sure is lookin' good. I never seen two gennlemen in blue be lookin' so good, y'know? Y'all sure are a pleasure to be aroun'. Hey, boss, you wanna see me dance? Betchall never seen no colored boy dances like I does. I sure does it good, too. All de white folks be sayin' so. (*He does a shuffle, using the broom as a prop. The* PIGS *clap time, and* UNCLE TOM *dances even harder. The* PIGS *tap time with their nightsticks.* TOM *still dances.*)

Hey, y'all wan' go head an' join me? Dis is fun, oh sir, it's fun, lawdy. (*The* PIGS *start to tap their toes.* UNCLE TOM *keeps dancing.*)

UNCLE TOM: Hey, y'all wanna see me turn aroun'? (*He does, using the broom as a pivot.*)

Hey, y'all wanna see me do my buck step? (*He puts the broom down and does a buck and wing. Then he slides into line with the* PIGS, *so that they're all in a straight line facing upstage. Something happens:* UNCLE TOM *pulls out two knives, and gently stabs the* PIGS *without them even knowing it. They slide dead to the stage floor.* UNCLE TOM *takes the knives out of the* PIGS' *bodies, and cleans them on his overalls. Then he picks up his broom.*)

Y'all know, it ain't what you do, it's how you do it. An' dat's a fack. (UNCLE TOM *goes offstage with the broom over his shoulder, loudly singing "Zip-A-Dee-Doo-Dah, Zipp-A-Dee-AAy," etc., etc.*)

BLACKOUT

El Teatro Campesino marching to the gravesite of Tibuercio Vasquez.

Graveyard ceremony for Vasquez.
(Luis Valdez in center foreground.)

Luis Valdez.

El Teatro performs *Los Vendidos*.

"I know your sign—you born under the sign of the Tom, with rope rising." The Bodacious Buggerrilla's *Uncle Tom*.

From *Uncle Sam* skit, the Bodacious Buggerrilla.

Miss America and Uncle Sam.

The San Francisco Mime Troupe concludes a show at San
Francisco's Civic Center, September 1971.

A performance of *Telephone* by the Mime Troupe.

Dear Nancy

Story: Once I was in Detroit, where I spent my time hanging out in the neighborhood bars. On my way home one morning from the Chesterfield on John R., I watched a pimp and a hooker having an argument in a parking lot. There he was in his silk suit, wide-brim hat, two-tone shoes, and gold and diamond jewelry. His Caddie Eldorado was parked at a rakish angle, and the stereo system inside was blasting Aretha. The hooker, in red dress and spike heels, was into a whole trip about what a no good prick he was. He was into his "you're a cunt and you'll straighten out your act or lose your face" spiel. A bitter, real-life game going on. The dialog was the same—almost line for line—as a script by the Bodacious Buggerrilla called *Killer Joe*. Is art life or is it vice versa?

Ed Bereal tells me that once the theater played *Killer Joe* in Watts, and right afterward, the real thing walked in the door. People, he says, just broke up. The cat would flash his cuffs, check out the soles of his shoes, make sure that his fly was up—and with each of those stylized moves, the crowd would break up even more. He finally split, because he couldn't get his shit together any more. Not with that audience—the Buggerrilla had shown them exactly what the pimp's game was, and they were ready for it, and combated it with exactly the right weapon: ridicule.

Bereal says that the Buggerrilla exists to show black people about themselves. I can believe it. But I think he's selling himself and the theater short. We've been playing two shows a night at the Ash Grove this past week (I say "we" because I'm now the token white in the group), and the audiences have been about sixty–forty young whites. Oh, the laughs come at different places than when I saw the Buggerrilla perform in Watts; but there is value—real heavy shock value—in what he's doing.

We've been doing *Threat to the Buggerrilla*, the skit we've put together for me. I come in at the beginning of the show and sit with the audience—usually with as straight a table of people as I can find. I'm in shirt and tie and jacket—the whole works. We all talk, and then the Buggerrilla comes on, and I watch for a while. The story is that I've just gotten a degree from a college in Orange County, and I'm a bit of a right-winger. Vietnam vet who believed in it and all that. I hate—HATE—the Buggerrilla. And I let my friends at the table know this in no uncertain terms.

"What are those damn boogies gonna do next" and that kind of stuff. Finally, after fifty-five minutes or so, one of the women in the theater comes out and starts to talk about the Buggerrilla. I've had enough, and I interrupt her. "Hey, enough. Wait a second. I've been listening to you people for like an hour now, and I just want you to know that you're really all wrong. You don't know what this country is all about. You people never do. All you can do is destroy our values, you know?"

Generally, folks tell me to shut up. But I continue (I'm just getting my shit together) with more talk. "Look, you guys are all wrong. I killed Commies in the Nam, you know? And some of my best friends there were colored like you, and they didn't ever talk this kind of crap. We all killed Commies together. It was real brotherly love in the Nam."

Anyhow, this kind of ad-lib goes on for like three minutes, and I keep getting more and more hot under the collar. People in the place get uptight, and they take sides—some saying shut up, others say let him talk. It's all for real. That's the frightening thing about it.

Okay, then I get really mad. The chick onstage is about to turn on me and go out, and I blow my top. I say, "This kind of thing has got to stop—it really has to stop because you're destroying America"— and I fumble in my pocket and pull out a Colt .38 and I shoot the chick on stage.

Immediately, I'm tackled and dragged out, and the lights go out. There's screams, and yells, and then all the lights go on, and there's the chick I shot all covered with blood standing in the light, and she says, "Welcome to the United States of Amerika."

Blackout.

It is dynamite, to say the least.

The first night we did it, we told nobody at the Ash Grove, and only the cats who would tackle me, and the chick I was to shoot. Two guys in the theater almost asked me outside during the middle of the gag, and a cat in the kitchen grabbed a knife and was gonna come after me with it.

Ed, of course, was happy as a kid with a free ice cream cone. Me too, for that matter. It's good theater—provocative, to say the least. And when I return to the straight table, I see that the skit has an effect on people. "You can't take anybody for what they are, can you?" said one girl. I told her that's the point of it. And that she should trust the cats in Sacramento and Washington about as much as she did me—after I shot somebody.

"Everybody's got a hustle," I say. "Just watch out for it. Use your head. That's what this thing is about."

That's the key to the Buggerrilla's kind of theater. They do shows about the classic Amerikan hustles—the dollar game played by Uncle Sam, the church hustle, the pimp, the revolutionary bullshit, the farce of politics—all behind a façade of laughter. The theater never seems to take any definite stand except "freedom." They're antidope and anticrime, and for the community asserting itself; but Bereal wants to indicate the problem more than he pushes any sort of concrete solution.

"That's what's called layin' freedom on people," he says. "Give 'em the knowledge that a hustle is a hustle, and then they have a choice. Accept it for what it is, or tell who's ever doin' it to fuck off, because you're onto his whole game."

Now, white audiences react differently to his stuff than black audiences. Somehow, get a group of whites in a room, and get black people doing some heavy theater and using words like nigger and coon, and there's a lot of nervous laughter. It's like I can read their minds—there they are, out for an evening of fun, having a pitcher of beer and impressing some broad, and then some black cat calls his brother a coon. Now, most of the people at the Ash Grove—the whites, anyway—are either longhairs or liberals or both. And they've been conditioned not to laugh at that kind of thing. But it's funny. So they laugh and feel guilty. Or they laugh and look nervously over their shoulder to see if the black dudes in the audience are laughing, too. They figure if the black dudes are having fun, it's all right. And if they're not, it would be safer to shut up.

A lot of the time, white kids will come backstage after the show and ask about the characters. Like Killer Joe—they'll ask if he's for real, simply because a pimp like that is strictly outside the normal white kid's frame of reference.

I think that the performances at the Ash Grove are intensely valuable because Bereal and the Buggerrilla are opening a lot of eyes whose only insight to the black street community has been *Shaft* or *Soul on Ice* or *Manchild in the Promised Land.* And if that's not laying freedom on people, I don't know what is.

We're going to rehearse for a while before tonight's show—there are a couple of new insults I want to put in before I pull the pistol out, and I'm not sure where they should go yet.

Love,

j

KILLER JOE

KILLER JOE: You girls don't have to fret or cry
You don't have to dream no mo'
'Cause I'm gon' handle all of that
That's right, my name is KILLER JOE!

Some think my momma was a Hurricane
And my daddy the Atom Bomb. . . .
But I created myself, myself, out of
The universal come!!!

I can snatch the eyebrows right off of death
And slap him off his feet. . . .
And if I find I'm short of cash,
Mother Nature's ass goes in the street!

I can fly from shore to shore,
Just to count the grains of sand. . . .
I can whip titties on the Lone Ranger, baby,
Put a pussy on Superman!

Oh yeah, don't nobody mess around with me,
Or be messing round my dough. . . .
'Cause when I get pissed off, my man,
Even the sun better come up slow!

There are some things that I have known, I've always under-
stood . . .
Without the proper man to love there is no womanhood.
You can do your thing and jive yourself, but really never know . . .
How to flow like the river Nile . . . screaming "RIDE IT, KILLER
JOE. . . ."
Hey, come on up here and take my arm or meet me in the basement.
My main lady needs a rest. . . . I need a spring replacement.

HOME BOY: KILLER JOE!!! Hey man, do you look bad. . . . Get down . . . shoes, socks, suit. Wow! Brother, you are out of sight (*improvised dialogue*) . . . And how you doin', my man?

KILLER JOE: Runnin' and funnin'—creepin' and sleepin'
Chewin' and screwin'—ressin' and dressin'.
I'm as slick as I want to be, ain't nobody's sucka. . . .
And if you touch my suit again, nigga
You'll be a dead mothafucka. . . .

HOME BOY (*dialogue improvised*): Didn't mean to touch you Killer, but wow! I get so excited I forget. . . . Brother, you are really out of sight. . . . Dynamite. . . . (*pressing too close to* JOE) Man, you must rilly be makin' it. . . . Hum man, huh? . . . Wow!

KILLER JOE: The fact that I let you stand up here talking to me . . .
Is somethin' that anyone walkin' by here can see. . . .
You ain't seen a blind man go by here ridin' or walkin'
So you ain't got to stand all up on me (*trying to be seen*) just cause
   we here talkin'! (*pause*).

You see that sun beam. Hey man do you see?
That particular beam of sunlight belongs just to me. . . .
Keep out of my sunshine or we gon' surely battle
Get your own sunbeam, nigga, and get off my shadow. . . .

HOME BOY: Sorry rilly man. . . . But whoa. . . . What are you into? What's happenin', what are you doin' for yourself? You all fine and sharp and all!!! Wow!!

KILLER JOE: A little stealin'—a little dealin'
A lots of leanin'—always feinin'
Super cokin'—lots of smokin'
Like the mornin' the principal walked in a-limpin'
Let every trick rest assured, that Killer Joe is still a-pimpin'.

HOME BOY (*loud, touching, excited*): Wow! Joe . . . you're too much. Same ole Joe. Wow!!!

KILLER JOE: Nigga, you're a chump for this man,
You been bought, worked and sold.
You're weird . . . too loud . . . touching my clothes.
You're goin' to meet with strife . . .
At the blade of my big knife. . . .
Make a widow of your wife
Touch me again and lose your life. . . .

And we might as well git it all straight
Never to be forgotten. . . .
Don't say nothin' else to me louder than a
Small cat pissin' onto cotton.

HOME BOY: Go Killer!!! (*checks self*) Too loud. . . . Wow, Killer,
you're out of sight. . . . Too much. . . . Go 'head, nigga!!!!
(*Turns* JOE *onto himself and women in audience.*) Go 'head, Killer,
pull 'em brother, pull 'em!

KILLER JOE (*to members of the audience*): Hey "Sweetmeat"
My sign is called CLITORIS, the bump that's in the boat
I give out love for days, Miss Fine, so to set your hips afloat. . . .
Is there a Scorpio lady anywhere in here . . . a Scorpio around?
I mean a natural Hotten Tot, with ass that's world renown. . . .
One of you fine things out there, come on now, raise your hand. . . .
My name is Dr. Feel Real Good, and I rule the lovin' land. . . .
The money's good and you can see, I'm fine from my head down
   to my feet. . . .
Tryin' to keep you Scorpios from givin' away what they sellin' down
   the street.

HOME BOY: A New Nigga. . . . Did you hear that . . . God damn
. . . a new nigga! Joe . . . take me in with you, man. . . . I sho'
would like to make some money like you. . . . Show me how to
pull a Libra brother, I've always be crazy for Libras. . . . Come
on, take me in with you, man . . . huh? Man . . . huh?

KILLER JOE: Ah! Yeah. . . . My shoeshine boy told me somethin'
Just for you . . . and it'd be real swell. . . .
Why don' you go do somethin' for yourself, they're
hirin' at Taco Bell (*punches* HOME BOY *away*).

(HOME BOY *begins to laugh.*)

KILLER JOE: I know you all black now and tryin' to be proud. . . .
But nigga, you still talkin' too much and laughin' too loud!
A greasy-faced nigga with teeth like a rat. . . .
What on earth could you find that you could laugh at?

HOME BOY (*laughing hysterically*): You're all fine Joe!!! Here
you driving a '71 Volkswagen. . . . You'll tear your suit gettin' into
that thing, man. . . . You can't get no whores in no Volkswagen.
. . . (*laughs.*)

KILLER JOE: Nigga, you loud and foul and liver-lipped, as we all can
see. . . .
Smellin' like garlic and Ripple and laughin' at me. . . .
I'm gonna tell you something, and it's a natural fact. . . .
It's niggas like you that be holdin' me back. . . .
You look like me, brother . . .
But that's where it all ends. . . .
You one of my low-life nigga friends. . . .
I never say Volkswagen, fool,
You must be totally insane. . . .
Them Ripple fumes musta taken root down deep in your brain. . . .
Now, you see how I'm dressed . . .
The pleats, the bottons, and the tuck . . . ?
Nigga, there's class sittin' out on that street. . . .
Check me and match it all up!!!

HOME BOY: White-on-white, in white. . . . (*dialogue describing
the Cadillac El Dorado.*)

KILLER JOE: You ain't no lizart, tell me . . . what is it?

KILLER JOE: ⎱ The white-on-white . . .
HOME BOY: ⎰

KILLER JOE: In Mink . . . El D . . .
Nigga, look no further. . . .
You found it. . . . That's me. . . .
(*Shaking car keys in* HOME BOY's *face.*)

HOME BOY: . . . And I know them payments must be kickin' your ass. . . . Ha! . . . Ha! . . .

KILLER JOE: Shit, financin' . . . loanin'
That shit's a crime. . . .
Mom's raised her son right . . .
One payment . . . One time. . . .

(*Enter* JIM HONKIE *"Paradise Finance" with a large* PIG *and snatches the car keys from* JOE.)

HOME BOY: Hey man, don't be doin' that to Joe man! No touchin' or talkin' too loud. . . . 'Cause Joe will pop you right in your mouth, Honkie! In fac', I just might pop you myself. Should I hit him, Joe? Should I, man?

(*All up on* JOE *again.*)

KILLER JOE (*put off by presence of the* PIG): Nigga evaporate, vanish, nigga disappear.
(*To* JIM HONKIE): Honkie, I just have this to say. . . .
(*To* HOME BOY, *who's back in the middle of things*): Nigga, get away from here. . . .

(JIM HONKIE, *in improvised dialogue, declares that* JOE *is behind in his payments and proceeds to repossess the car, leaving.*)

HOME BOY: OOOOOHWHEEEE. . . . Nigga, they done took your ride (*laughs*), and you spoozed to be bad, but I guess ain't no nigga too awful bad when it comes to Whitey. . . . You be kickin' death's ass, fuckin' mother Nature. . . . Your daddy is a Atom Bomb, but when it comes to Whitey you ain't shit. . . . (*laughs hysterically.*)

KILLER JOE: There you go, see there you go, being too loud
Makin' a scene and causin' a crowd
Hey, I don't be worried about that Peck
Comin' up here and talkin' all out the side of his neck. . . .
Shiiiiiit . . . takin' that Punkie El D ain't no kinda stopper.
I'm a space-time nigga, I'm gonna get me a helicopter!

HOME BOY: Wow . . . go 'head, Killer. . . . Wow, brother, you're too much, loose a 1972 white-on-white in mink El Dorado and it ain't nothin', huh. . . . Is it, Killer . . . is it . . . huh . . . is it? . . . White boy take your car and it ain't shit, huh?

KILLER JOE: Shiiiiiit . . . I'm not too upset, as anyone here can see 'Cause it was the honkie's wife that gave the car to me. . . . But check me out, man, the suit, the rings, the hat and such. Now on the objective side, ain't I too much?

HOME BOY: Go, Joe . . . a new nigga, I'm old, I ain't shit, but this is a new nigga, nothing on earth before like him, work Joe, teach us . . . Shiiiiiit. . . .

(*Re-enter* JIM HONKIE *with* PIG, *warning officer about how dangerous victims can be the second time around.* JIM HONKIE *accuses* JOE *of being behind on the payments for his jewelry.*)

KILLER JOE (*to* PIG): Hey Home . . . that's my birthstone.

JIM HONKIE: No, that's our birthstone! ! !

(JIM HONKIE *talks about possible financing of jewelry as he starts to leave. Notices ledger and the old two-name game. Payment behind on suit also. Forces* KILLER JOE *to give up his suit right there on the street.*)

KILLER JOE: I don't give up my suit, I don't care who you are. You don't pull with the suit what you pulled with the car.

JIM HONKIE: Listen, fella, do you want to give us the suit here or do we take a little ride down to the glass house, it's up to you. . . . Just tell me what it's going to be.

HOME BOY: You don't have to stand for this, Joe. . . . You got your rights, you can sue them for every penny they got. . . . You can fight this through courts, all the way to the Supreme Cou—

(PIG *hits him with billy club, shuts him up.*)

KILLER JOE: See you gone and fooled around and got me real pissed. And I'll have to see that your wife hears about this.

JIM HONKIE: Look, I don't have a lot of time, do I get the suit or don't I?

KILLER JOE (*Giving in and throwing the coat to* JIM HONKIE, *only after sneaking his gun to* HOME BOY): I been much too easy on you, I can see it all now
You ain't getting no more pussy, honkie, not at home anyhow
Here, take this suit, you jivin' ole Jew
I just wear my shit once anyhow, then I'm through.

JIM HONKIE: Let's take a little walk through the dictionary, fella. . . . Now, a suit consists of two parts. . . . I'm holding one part and you're still wearing the other.

HOME BOY: Killer, no man, you don't have to give up your pants, man. . . .

(PIG *makes threatening gesture and shuts him up*).

JIM HONKIE: Of course, there's always the glass house. . . .

KILLER JOE: Look man, we can—

JIM HONKIE: Please, please, I never conduct business on the street, come around to the office in the morning and I'll see what we can work out. . . . And now, our pants, please. I think I can see that the officer is getting a little impatient. . . .

KILLER JOE: This don' mean shit. . . . Does everybody hear? THIS DON' MEAN SHIT. . . . Everybody get it clear.
(*taking his pants off, speaking to* JIM HONKIE)
Just make it hard on yourself, go 'head make a revolutionary out of me!
'Cause I'm coming back in my African Robe to burn up every cashmere suit I see!
(HONKIE *and* OFFICER *begin to leave.*)

I'm gonna free Angela, honkie . . . walk right through your
   door. . . .
I make sure the revolution starts in your store.

HOME BOY (*trying to hide* JOE's *nakedness*): Hey brother, we gon'
have to get you off the streets, man. . . . You can't be out here like
this. . . . I mean, it just ain't natural. . . .

KILLER JOE: Shiiiiiiiit. . . . Ain't no big thang, and dig what I preach
Folks wear less than this right down in Palm Beach.
Some people smack changes, gets loose with the weather. . . .
My storehouse stays full of shit gets better and better.

(*Enter* WHORES, *who take one look at* JOE *and completely crack up.*)

KILLER JOE: Go 'head bitches, have your laugh, enjoy it if it's
   funny. . . .
But while your asses shake with the fun, get together all my
   money. . . .

HOME BOY (*after laughing with the girls, whispers to one of them*):
Think that's somethin', ask the nigga where the white-on-white
Cadillac El Dorado is. Ask him. . . . Just ask him. . . .

WHORE No. 1: Yeah, Joe, where's the ride? I was the one who laid
up night after night on my back and paid for that ride. . . . Where's
the car, Mr. Slick Nigga? . . .

HOME BOY (*talking to* JOE): Oooooooohwwhheeeee. . . . I don't
even want to see this, oh my God! ! ! Joe . . . Joe, don't do it, Joe,
don't kill her, Joe, don't kill her. . . . Just give her one more chance,
bro—it's not worth it, don't kill her . . . don't, Joe. . . .

KILLER JOE: Bitch, hand me my money or I'll make your head knotty
Make me slap all the water right out of your body.

HOME BOY (*again on* WHORE's *side*): That ain't shit, is it, baby? That
ain't nothin' . . . show us! ! !

WHORE No. 1: That ain't gon' git it Joe! Naw, baby, not at all,
But let me say it to you so you'll understand it. . . .
This morning the man I left behind . . . was cold and slick and very
    fine
I'm back and his shit is very raggedy
Your draws is gone you're looking faggedy
Now I know I'd be a piss po' whore . . .
If I gave a sissy my whore'n dough
Naw nigga, you'll have to learn how to beg
Or sell you own crooked skinny-ass leg. (*Exit* No. 1.)

HOME BOY (*back on* JOE's *side, shoot at* WHORE No. 1 *as she leaves*):
That's okay bitch, you never were hittin' on nothin'. Funny-lookin'
whore. . . . *Leave me!* . . . Ain't no love lost . . . oh no! Shiiit,
ain't hardly no kinda big thang!

KILLER JOE (*to* HOME BOY): I would make it rhyme, but I don't have
the time. Three words to you should really do it. SHUT UP
NIGGA!!!!!

(*Turns to* WHORE No. 2, *talks excitedly*) My main lady, standin'
    here just lookin' out for me.
Baddest sister for miles around, as anyone can see.

WHORE No. 2: Joe, Joe . . . you're too loud . . . standing on
my shadow . . . and you're touching my clothes. . . . You know
better than that. . . .

KILLER JOE: Now baby, I've always been sweet and you know I've
    been kind. . . .
I bought you those furs, makin' sure you was fine.
I taught you the game; how to sniff the best coke. . . .
Introduced you to diamonds and all the best folk. . . .

HOME BOY (*to* WHORE No. 2): He lost the jewelry too. . . . Sure
did. . . .

KILLER JOE (*to* WHORE No. 2): I gave you my arm so that you could
    be seen

While your money was cool you were always my queen.
(*gets angry*)
But hand me some cash or my foot goes in your hips. . . .

WHORE No. 2 (*pulls out a gun and puts it right up to* JOE's *mouth*):
Yeah nigga and seventeen bullets go deep in your lips. . . . Little
jive time, off the wall, bubble-gum pimp. . . . (*excitedly*) You little
skinny-leg popcorn, jive-time sucker . . . kiss my ass. . . .

KILLER JOE: That's okay, you skankie whore, but you better look in
them flabs . . .
'Cause last nite I just gave you a bad case of crabs. . . .

HOME BOY (*to excited* WHORE): GET OUT! ! ! I mean, get out. . . .
Your money was always funny. . . . That's that women's liberation
shit. . . . I hope them crabs turn into old Volkswagens.

KILLER JOE: SHUT UP, NIGGA . . . I'm always covered in silk or in
leather. . . .
I said my shit's good it's always together
Now stand close to me and do a slow lean
And I'll show you a roll of very long green.

KILLER JOE *pulls a roll of bills from under his shirt, and while he
sneakily shows it to* HOME BOY, HOME BOY *hits him over the head
several times, takes* JOE's *money, his hat, shoes, and starts to leave.
He goes back after counting the money, hits* JOE *a couple more
times for not having more, and again starts to leave.*

HOME BOY: Sorry Joe, but everybody's got to have a hustle!

(*Exits.*)

Journal: Sunday

Met with Bereal this morning to talk over some things: the success of the show at the Ash Grove, the Buggerrilla, and Bereal.

We taped the conversation on the mike Bereal has hanging over the table—he tapes just about everything. Asked him afterward if I could borrow and transcribe the tape, to see if we were making any sense. From the look of it we were.

E.: Well you know, I started out a really precocious child; for one reason or another, art just popped out of my hands. I couldn't pick up anything without doin' it in, you know? Not to say that it was fantastic stuff, it was just done by a kid. But I just couldn't help build stuff and draw stuff. Even to the point of warping me in the sense that I thought art was born and not created or made, you know? I thought either you did it from the cradle or maybe you did a truck driver thing from the cradle, and that's what you were, you know? But me, man, I never knew nothin' else but doin' art. In fact, I got kept back in the third grade because at one point I said fuck it, I just want to draw. I don't want to do any of that other stuff, I just want to draw.

Hey, you know, I can tell you about grade school experience that you can't even start to believe, man. You won't believe it. Like I was in a country town, in a ghetto, Riverside, California. And in the fifties it was strange. It was a tight Mexican-American-black community, you know, and in the grade school I went to, man, it was fuckin' dangerous and weird in that all the teachers there were the castoffs of society. So we got freaks, man. We got flagellists and sadists. Look, one of my best buddies, man, went over to the field right next to the school and got a gopher snake, got a four-foot gopher snake, man. He was runnin' around chasin' people with it, right? The principal, man, pulled him into his office, took the gopher snake, and beat him with it. I had to walk into the office after it was over. Every time he hit the kid he snapped the tail off the snake, so there was fuckin' blood all over. Gross, you know. Imagine gettin' whipped with a snake. The kid that got whipped went on to kill a coupla guys, man. And today he's gone, snapped out.

We had a lady instructor in sixth grade who would get off and tell you how babies are born and have you come over and rub her stomach. Wow, very strange shit. Or there was a young chick who used to like to sit at a desk; she had a open-front desk, and she'd open her legs, do a whole number. She'd sit the older boys in a position so they could check her legs out. She dug watchin' them watch her. You know, I mean it was that kind of weird. Very, very very strange.

Anyway, that was pretty much the realm I had to live in. But I was paintin' pictures too, and that was my in to a certain extent. In any case I went through all that, went through junior high school, high school, and went into art school, which was like the real turn-on, 'cause I met a coupla guys who really took my head and turned me on. And then I split to San Francisco, worked on my own, split to New York for a while and worked on my own, came back here, and set up a studio.

J.: Were you making any bread?

E.: A gallery was paying me like seven hundred dollars to stay home and paint pictures. They had a gallery in New York and another one in Paris, and I was beatin' *Time* magazine and *Life* magazine away from the door 'cause I was a commodity. It hung me up in the sense that I had been used to struggling doin' my stuff, and like to have the Easy Street kind of a thing and people knockin' at the door all the time sayin' "Is it ready yet" really hung me up bad. Kept me from workin' 'cause I never trusted the market. And it was really funny in the sense that by the time I had come out of art school I had a reputation already: Watch out for Bereal, man, talented, far-out dude, man, incredible, you know?

It was a nice go for a coupla years except it hung me up. The thing that brought all that to a close was 1965 and the Watts riots. I was like workin' fifteen, sixteen hours a day in the studio, and all of a sudden the streets came up my front walk and through the front door. One mornin' I got up, walked out on the front porch, and there was a machine gun, a .50-caliber machine gun pointed at the house and nine freaks in Army clothes, laughin' and gigglin' and strange. And I go, "Wait a minute; I forgot somethin'; hold it; stop it." So at that point I shut down the gallery. I shut down my studio, I shut down everything I was doin' and I started like givin' some consideration to what was goin' on. I really backed off a long way. That's what dropped me off into the theater thing 'cause I had been writing and a bunch of shit, you know.

J.: Does that mean that whole relationship where your art gets suddenly thrust into life?

E.: Yeah, because it's like a never-never land; it's like a whirlpool in the sense that it feeds on itself. You don't need anybody, man, you know? You do your pictures; you're in a milieu. There are old, fashionable, wealthy ladies who don't know where they are; but it's fashionable to buy your stuff. It's fashionable to invite you to their house, have cocktails and you do somethin' weird, which increases your number, which sends you back, and you do another picture and then you come out to the cocktail party again. You do somethin' weird for them and give them a little story to tell the rest of the week; and you make some bread off it because you sell 'em a whole piece: Here's a picture by the guy who just did the funny story I just told you, right. And everyone else goes OOOOOHHHHH and that leads to the next cocktail party, you know, and it just goes on and on and on like that; it don't mean nothin' at all. And all the time you are truckin' back to the ghetto to get some work done, and you never think I'm going back to the ghetto, you know; I Am Going Back To The Ghetto. And all your fellow ghetto residents are going wow, man, you have a heavy thing goin', wow, that's really heavy. And you even think you got a heavy thing going. And the little rich lady thinks she's got a heavy thing going. She say: Well, I know some people in the ghetto. And her friends say: Really? Wow, you know. . . .

It was really strange, man, it was really very strange. Because I suspect I can't know what it was really about; I kept blowing the scene to a certain extent 'cause I didn't believe in what I was doing, but I certainly didn't have enough information to expose the deal. And I thought I was doing a number which would rip off the rich cats. The thing is, though, if you put your hands in a sewer man, you're gonna get fuckin' dirty. That's all, regardless of how much you might not even call it a sewer, it's very fuckin' dirty. Shit is shit. I think probably you get a part of it; I get it to a great extent—when I realize that I'm bicultural, you know, and like there's a part of you going hey wait a minute; there's another life. And a lot of stuff that guys are saying yeah yeah yeah about is *not* yeah yeah yeah, 'cause I know a better way to do that; it's not a *kosher* way to do that; but it's a *better* way, and it's pullin' at me. You know, it's like sayin' wait a minute, there's other levels of reality.

J.: Well, that shows you were into the process of going from that whole scene into people's theater, starting to relate the kind of shit that you see every day. Like when I said that people's theater takes reality and distorts it to a comic-book level to show the facts.

E.: See, that art realm exists but society cools it out and all the sensitive guys, man, they're gone. They become no good because it gets to be art for art's sake.

J.: Or art for money's sake.

E.: Yeah, which is essentially the same thing. In that if you're not creating with a purpose, it doesn't mean anything. It doesn't challenge anything. But it's extremely cultural—in the sense that it's white cultural. But you have people who are disenfranchised, you got a court system, man, that's incredibly vicious. You got guys who have no alternative between armed robbery and eating, man, you know? And at the same time you've got artists doing what's called minimal art—you take a shiny chrome bar—seven feet long—and you put one point of the bar two feet from the corner of a white room and lean the other part into the carpet—Art, right? Now wait a minute, hold it. What does it fuckin' mean in relation to the human condition?

J.: It doesn't have anything to do with the human condition.

E.: Exactly. Now that is a hip way to cool people out, and that's what our realm is entirely about. So that at one point I started to feel wait a minute; art doesn't mean anything; I'm not doing anything. And that, together with the realization—shit, stoned realization that happened to me when I went over this whole thing—"I pledge allegiance to the flag of the United States of America, and to the republic for which it stands, one nation under God with liberty . . ."

J.: ". . . indivisible . . ."

E.: ". . . indivisible with liberty and justice for all???" And I mean, *really*, you know, and I went wait a minute—hold it, hold it, hold it, wait. That's not true, you know—and it was as dumb as that. Like you're goin' into your apartment or you're walking on the street and a cop comes up to you and calls you nigger, puts a .38 or a .357 magnum in the front of your head, and you're shakin', man, shiverin'. And you know that if he had a bad day with his wife or somethin', you're that far away. And you also know he kinda' wants to do it anyway. And you're goin', wait a minute—I went to Howard University, man, I got the paper at home. And he's goin', "You're a nigger, period." So at one point you go, "Hold it, wait a minute. Wait, wait, wait, wait, wait a minute. It's not true; it's not happening." And you start—you're forced—to develop your own kind of reality. You start to search, man, and everything's up for grabs. What you get from that is the knowledge that it's possible to play the game and not get dirty—you think. Which isn't so. Niggers are niggers, whether or not they've gone to Howard University, and the man is still gonna' blow 'em away if he wants to. So you learn to go 'round that. Catch what you need and split. 'Cause that's what the man is doin' to you if he can. Like for example we been at the Ash Grove for this week, right?

J.: Yeah.

E.: Well, here's one thing that came out of that. There were some cats from a TV network and they said, "Hey, we want to do a number and really feature you guys. The thing we wanna do is, like, do Uncle Tom. Only we don't wanna see Uncle Tom ruining himself by rippin' off pigs at the end of the play. Just the image of Uncle Tom —that's what we want on television." Shit. You go, "Wait a minute, man. This is 1971, you know, it isn't 1951. Come on." And they say, "Oh yeah, I see your point. Well, we'll call you," and they split. The cats want to grab your baddest shit and split with it. But then they gotta do it over, because they don't know how to deal with it. Now when we do our shit in front of a group of black people, we're comin' from "Okay—this is the information intellectually." The basic stuff might be from Mao, Marx—any number of people, you know. What we have to do is take that and translate it into a cultural kind of milieu so that it's digestible. You know, put it into a form where people will dig it and say yeah, great idea.

J.: They don't have to know that it's Karl Marx or Mao. . . .

E.: Yeah, and frankly for me, fuck that. Does it work, does it alleviate my situation at all? That's what's important, man. I don't give a fuck who it is. Look, one of the things that's far out is Karl Marx or Mao or Malcolm or Marcus Garvey or Langston Hughes, all those guys had information; sometimes it simply wasn't coded quite right.

J.: Yeah, well, who were they writing for?

E.: You know, exactly. A lot of times, I'll tell you, a lot of the things that I rebel against on that whole art scene is like art for art's sake. A lot of the freedom talk has been for freedom's sake only, too. It's been talking to history and not to the people. It's like hey, will my name drop off into history properly, you know; and a lot of the information has been good, righteous information. It has simply not been directed to the people. Now, can we take information, reinterpret it, translate it, transpose it into a way that we can run it to the people and they go, "Oh baby, hey, I dig that." It's the difference between saying, "Hey, dig it: Oppressed, Third World people throughout the world have got to unite against imperialists, capitalist domination" and saying, "Hey, man, dig it, you're gettin' ripped off; you gotta get yourself together. You gotta get yourself not only together with you and your kind, but you gotta get yourself together with Mexican cats, Japanese cats—not only here but everyplace." The cat can say hey, man, I dig that.

J.: What that is, is when the theater does things right—which means without intellectualizing it or anything, really abstruse concepts become beautifully palatable. But really, what the Buggerrilla's talking about is freedom. Like that old thing of laying freedom on people. Doing it in simple terms. Which is dangerous, no?

E.: Right, man. Like in the film *Easy Rider* they made a statement that I was very impressed with. It was that one thing terrorizes the United States of America more than anything else, and that is the concept of freedom. People will kill you for that, man. And if you not supposed to have it, oh, wow. I mean—like niggers free? That's a trip. If niggers were free, man, Uncle Sam couldn't run his game on 'em. Or on anybody else, either. Like—like I remember when I was teaching art at the University of California. In the morning I taught at Irvine, in the afternoon at Riverside. Morning was called white upper-middle-class, bread, all those things; afternoon was called guys out from the street into school, all black, right? And in a day it's a trip; it's a trip, man. The first day I walked into Irvine, all the kids were sitting on the floor around the tallest chair in the room, waiting. You know, like they knew that out of that chair there are gonna be some words that are gonna make it like okay, and I just couldn't believe it, man, and they didn't know it was me teaching the course.

What I did was go into the back of the room and join them. Went to the back of the semicircle and joined 'em, you know, and sat down and waited for somebody to show up; and everyone's looking around and I'm looking around too. And I start talkin' to the guy next to me, you know, and he asks me what my major was and I said I didn't have one and he said how can you be here not having a major. And I said, "I teach here, I'm an instructor," and he said, "What do you instruct?" I said, "This class." And then everybody starts, like it starts moving, you know, all the group of people making it half time. And I say, "WOW, you guys are far fuckin' out. Wow, you know, look at me. Do I really belong in that chair, man? Wow, you guys really made a hell of a statement. You made a stronger statement sitting around that chair than you're gonna make all year on a piece of paper." (It was a drawing class.) I says, "Wow, man, are we gonna have a hard time," and I proceed to tell 'em, "I want to lay freedom on you guys, and you guys are gonna cry. You're gonna be uncomfortable. You're gonna be really in trouble, man." And you know, at that point I flashed on the ghetto. Wow.

J.: 'Cause it's a ghetto as much as anything else?

E.: Oh, man, trouble, really in trouble. Layin' freedom on folks is a real trip, you know? Because they were really in trouble—they were really hung up intellectually about art. No soul, man, just book learning.

J.: And that's the whole thing; that's where my book is at, man. You can't write it down; you can't do that shit. You gotta either *do* it or let the people who do it talk about it.

E.: Yeah, yeah.

J.: Because otherwise you . . .

E.: . . . destroy it and it becomes somethin' else.

J.: Yeah, it becomes—it becomes a treatise on something, you know it becomes . . .

E.: . . . very safe, man, right, very safe to talk about.

J.: Right. And the whole thing about guerrilla theater is that it can be done by anybody. . . .

E.: . . . who wants to take a position on where this fuckin' country is off to.

J.: Exactly. It don't take a bunch of angry black people to do it— it could be anybody.

E.: Which is what is cool about *Threat to the Buggerrilla*. See, where the whites couldn't relate to us because of the material, they could relate to you. You were just a guy voicing his opinion—until you pulled out the .38.

J.: Yeah. And that's what made it work for me, too. It would bring it home to the white folks because I was white, and they'd decide to stay, and we'd talk about the theater for a while. And what I found out was they'd say, "What really got to us was that you were so real. And if *you* were for real, maybe the Buggerrilla's for real."

E.: OOOOOOOOHHHHHHH, I see.

J.: Like maybe if I, a white plant, could get up and shoot somebody, then what the theater's doin' ain't no minstrel show after all.

E.: Maybe it's real.

J.: And I said that's right. You should think about it.

E.: And when you go home and when you go back to Orange County tonight, think about it. Very, very heavy.

J.: Think about the fact that there are a lot of people around who are gonna have pieces in their pocket. Think about the fact that what I did tonight I—or anybody—could not only have done with the Buggerrilla, but I could have done it at a speech of Spiro Agnew's or George Wallace's.

E.: All it takes is a haircut and a tie. That's what must be very frightening. 'Cause obviously you sat there and like pulled 'em in; you sat there and you knew what to tell 'em. That must be very far out, because they're going for it, right? And all of a sudden the guy that they're really going for, who really personifies a lot of information that they think they got, all of a sudden turns out to be a whole other person.

J.: Yeah. What I said to them was hey, you know, all you gotta do is think. Just trust your intuition and be your own man. And that's where it's at. That's the whole idea of this thing.

E.: Very good, very good.

J.: Is be where you're at. Don't trust the left; don't trust the right. Don't trust anybody except you.

E.: Go for where you are, right.

J.: Go *from* where you are.

E.: Heavy. Very heavy.

J.: Friday night, there was a hero who got his hand shot, did you know that? I pulled out the piece, and there was a guy who reached for me, who was like sitting three chairs away, and he lunged and grabbed for me, and caught the muzzle blast in the hand. And he went around afterward saying, "Oh gee, man, somebody killed me."

E.: That's why, in most cases, that's why we put our people around everybody, and, you know, not only do we grab you to make it that real, but it's also protection. Because the minute you shoot her, man, you're gonna be hit by six guys; but you're safe.

J.: You know—pull the piece out, and then fire, and then do a relaxation exercise.

E.: Yeah, that's right. 'Cause it's really heavy. That's one of the best things that goes down, and we always have to be very careful where we do that because there are some areas where we cannot do that thing at all.

J.: Right, because if there's somebody who just happens . . .

E.: Yeah, right.

J.: The only thing I was worried about was at the Ash Grove, some idiot narc.

E.: Yeah, right. Because there were a lot of them in the Grove . . . there were a coupla very obvious guys . . .

J.: Oh, they were so obvious, like one guy says, "I hope you find your way to the commune, man." Yeah, it was just so ridiculous.

E.: Hey, remember that time I told you about when we did *Killer Joe* in Maverick Flats here in our community. We just did the whole number, finished it up, and man, Killer Joe walked in the place for real, right? And he was lookin' Baad, you know? And everybody's laughin', and he is standin' there trying to find out who they're laughin' at, and it's him. And then he tried to, like, outdo 'em; but there's too many people, man, just crackin' up. He's really in trouble and he's just kinda' goin' wow, I'm naked. Incredible, incredible, man. 'Cause little did he know what had just gone down; we just saw you, man, I mean you know. What we did was, we got into that cat's game, and laid a little freedom on all the people that used to think his act was real.

J.: But people say, "Hey, what do you mean, 'freedom.'" You know, if you were in any other country, you'd be locked up for saying what you're saying. What do you say? Answer me, answer me.

E.: I can tell you, I can tell you. The only reason we can say what we say is because the powers that be right now are very confident that they can co-opt it; if they can't co-opt it out front with so-called justice, then they rip you, rip you. They'll do one of several things. They'll either buy you off, draft you, or threaten you. Now, if those three covert methods don't work, they'll go to overt methods. It's that simple. Now, one way—we always see it from the government or the papers, which protects the status quo—they'll say, "Don't listen to him, he's a kook—a freak."

J.: But you see on the covert level, which is more insidious and more dangerous, it happens that hey the Bodacious Buggerrilla has just received a twenty-five-thousand-dollar grant from the National Endowment on the Arts.

E.: Exactly, or the Ford Foundation or whatever.

J.: That's how good old Uncle Sam does it.

E.: Yeah. Uncle Sam's got to effect where they're comin' from, you know, "Come here, come here, I like what you're sayin', that's good. Talks about freedom. Talks about democracy. Talks about power for the people, let Old Uncle Sam in, I like it. Take this, let me give you a little money to do what you're doin'. Let me give you some personnel; let me help you; you got a mailing list you gotta get out, let me give you some people to help you, you know. Let me do this; let me do that. Hey, look, I got a suggestion: Maybe it would be more effective if it's gone, it's over."

J.: Which is why the Campesino isn't taking grants these days.

E.: Sure. If they don't want to get sucked into Sam's game, they can't. But what really knocked me out about those Chicano cats is how into their people they really are. I mean, it's like an incredibly real people's theater.

J.: Exactly. People can do it. Theater . . .

E.: . . . is where you find it. You're doin' it every day. Now, theater might be the key to the other arts. Because I suppose poetry talks about the way to talk; I think the graphic arts talk about the way to look; theater encompasses all of that and more—which says that it might be talking about how to live. You see, because I suspect if you really get it together, there is no more painting; there is no more sculpture; there is no more poetry. We just live and we dig it in each other. So that when this guy talks you go, "Oh, hey, man, that was really hip." Or when this guy says, "Hey, you know what I see, man, I see this, this, this, and this," you go, "That's a beautiful picture."

J.: What you're doing then is removing it from that whole intellectual trip.

E.: And getting it on a simple level, you know? On a you-and-I living day-to-day level. Because otherwise I think we're just fuckin' with each other. I think men have been jiving each other for a long time. Like you know, hey, how can I get the ideal Greek cat to sit still, look like marble and stand on a pedestal? Now, I suspect a Greek statue would be hipper if you could talk to it, man; and ask it to take another pose, do other numbers. And if it'll fart—you know if you can get the Venus de Milo to fart, man, I think that's an issue. To say to Venus, "Now, if I could get you to fart, I could rap with you a little bit." Now, the point is can we take theater out of the test tube, off the stage, and get it down where you can and I can talk about it. Which is all saying that the statue ain't no hipper than me. I am alive; there's life in me. I have life in me and I'm sitting here admiring death. You know I'm admiring a thing that don't move, that don't do anything. Fuck that. Cut the muthafucker off its pedestal and let *me* stand up there; I'll rap with you. To take it a step further, fuck the pedestal. You know, talk to me directly. That's what the Buggerrilla is all about.

J.: Fucking pedestals?

E.: Yeah, do it—laundrymats, laundrymats. Beautiful place to have the theater. Theater goes on. All I'm tryin' to tell ya' is if I walk in in a funny face and a wild costume, all I'm tryin' to say is ultimately, there is theater. Get it together, you know. Or in the supermarket or wherever. It goes on. Now, if that's the given, where is our sculpture? Where is our poetry? Where is our theater? Where is our music, man? Why not get it all back to where they really are? I can touch you in that I can be an actor, I can be me, I can be me, I can be her; I can be any number of things for whatever purpose. But it's not to be confused with the thing happenin' between you and I, which is real; the thing that happens onstage up there, which might be the information you really wanna talk about, is not real. That's up there, but, you know, "ha ha ha ha ha. Of course that's not possible."

J.: Hey, if I'm talking to you and you're real, maybe they out there . . .

E.: Exactly. *They* are real and the stage is just a cover, because you gotta be covered to keep from getting shot. Really, you know.

The East Bay Sharks.

The East Bay Sharks.

Audience participation in the East Bay Sharks.

The Street Player's Union performs
Smile on the Boston Common.

The Street Player's Union performs
Smile on the Boston Common.

New York's Soul and Latin Theater Company.

"I wish I had something to wish for," says a member of SALT.

City Street Theater, New York

Concept East performs *White Sale*. Photo by Michael Braynon.

1984

NARRATOR: Ladies and gentlemen: *1984*

White Side I

(*Opens with whites singing "America the Beautiful."*)

PECKERWOOD NO. 1: Boy, I'll be glad to get back. I missed breakfast this morning, and it's damn near lunchtime. . . . What are we supposed to have for lunch today, Chet?

PECKERWOOD NO. 2: I think Gary said we had a treat (*cough*) comin' today. They got some more of that synthetic porterhouse steak for today, I think!

PECKERWOOD NO. 3: Hey, that'll be great (*cough*). . . . If I have to eat another ham sandwich or pork chop today, I'll go out and kill one o' them niggers (*cough*) and eat him just for the change.

(*Flash of businessman.*)

PECKERWOOD NO. 2 (*laugh . . . cough*): Yeah, seems as though the only things that grows these days is pigs and niggers (*laugh . . . cough . . . laugh*).

PECKERWOOD NO. 1: I wonder if the niggers are having (*cough*) as much trouble with food and water as we are?

PECKERWOOD NO. 3: Don't laugh. . . . One of the guys down from Oakland out of interrogation said (*cough*) that . . . the niggers they capture tell them they eat roaches and rats as side dishes and white folks as the main course. . . . I think they call it . . . Cream of Southern Cracker (*cough*).

PECKERWOOD NO. 1: Gosh, race war is hell, ain't it?

(*All agree, and they push on, coughing.*)

Black Side I

BROTHER No. 1: Hey, man, you hear about the raid on Pacoima last night? We killed up a bunch of honkies (*cough*).

BROTHER No. 2: Wow, no, man. You think they might try again today?

BROTHER No. 1: What time is it, man? (*cough*).

BROTHER No. 2: Ahhhhhhhhh, almost noon (*cough, cough*).

BROTHER No. 1: Naw, not much chance of any trouble now, they'll probably be into eatin' lunch, that is, if you call all those little pills and shit that them eat lunch (*cough*).

BROTHER No. 3: Speaking of eating, man, I could sure use somethin' to eat myself (*cough . . . cough*).

BROTHER No. 4: Hey, you know what I wish I had? I wish I had me some collard greens, some black-eyed peas, and maybe some chittlins and rice (*cough*).

(*Flash of businessman.*)

BROTHER No. 5: Aw, man, you know there ain't been nothin' growin' for the past twelve or thirteen years. . . . If we hadn't stumbled on that frozen-food locker a few years back wouldn't nobody remember none of that kinda stuff (*cough . . . cough . . . cough*).

BROTHER No. 6: I was around during the time food was frozen. . . . What is collard greens and that other stuff that grows? (*cough . . . cough*).

White Side II

PECKERWOOD No. 2: You know, a friend of mine let me read this book he had. . . . It was written a long time ago about what they thought life would be nowadays. . . . Boy, were they off (*cough . . . cough*).

PECKERWOOD No. 3: What was the name of it, seems like I kinda remember that (*cough*).

PECKERWOOD No. 2: It was called *1984*. I forgot who wrote it (*cough . . . cough*).

PECKERWOOD No. 1: What do you mean, they were "off"?

PECKERWOOD No. 2: They mostly talk about the government, takin' over an' makin' people do what they want 'em to do and malarkey like that (*cough*), and everything is clean and antiseptic, sterile-like. . . .

(*All laughing, coughing, gagging . . . more laughing.*)

Clean? . . . Antiseptic? . . . Sterile? . . .

PECKERWOOD No. 3: You mean they don't even mention the niggers at all? Revolutions? Or the Mexicans or them damn factories with their gases or the deaths?

PECKERWOOD No. 1 (*coughing*): The fact that your eyes burn all the time or what you got to go through just to get a drink of water (*coughing violently*).

(*Flash of businessman.*)

PECKERWOOD No. 2: You better let the doc check you out (*cough*); your cough don't sound normal to me (*cough*). Not like mine or Barney's. . . . Have you been takin' your respiration shots every morning?

NARRATOR: *Members of each of these parties drop along the way as they push on. The dying of a friend or comrade by natural causes has become such a common occurrence these days that no one hardly notices.*

Black Side II

BROTHER No. 2: Hey, I'll bet I can remember something that you guys can't (*cough*). I can remember the sun and even clouds! (*cough, cough, cough, cough*).

BROTHER No. 4: Yeah, I can kinda remember that (*cough*). My mother used to tell me about somethin' called . . . ah . . . sunsets (*cough*).

BROTHER No. 1: That was when the air was almost fit to breathe and there was even fresh, clean water to drink . . . and birds and insects and stuff. . . .

(*Flash of businessman.*)

ALL: AH, COME ON, MAN, YOU'RE JIVIN'. WE DON'T BELIEVE THAT, MAN, SHIT, C'MON!!!!!

BROTHER No. 1: Really, man it was rilly nice . . . it wasn't like what happened to Joe the other day. . . . The brother forgot and went in to take a bath while he was smokin' . . . you all know how bad the chemicals are in the water. . . . He blew himself right up. . . .

BROTHER No. 3: I'm not sure I'd rather not drink Ripple than water anyhow.

BROTHER No. 5: There used to be light . . . not electric lights, but real . . . natural light . . . from nature, and there were things like stars, and the moon and folks were all healthy all the time! (*continued coughing*).

BROTHER No. 6: Really, wow, that's hard to believe, I can't remember no time when it wasn't dark or when we wasn't fightin' them honkies. . . . How did it all get like this? Ain't there some folks who can afford the sun even nowadays? (*continued coughing*).

BROTHER No. 3: Oh yeah, there's a few who can afford to live all year 'round in a space satellite above all this shit . . . just come down once in a while for spare parts or life-support machinery (*cough, cough*).

BROTHER No. 6 (*cough*): But how did it all start? . . .

NARRATOR: 1984 . . . How did it all start? By the mid-seventies most countries of the world found themselves thoroughly overrun by their own numbers; population growth was completely out of control. Even though wars were contrived by their governments, the ranks of the people grew.

In the United States of America, because there were ever-increasing numbers of factories, machines, and profits for some, there was increasing unemployment, poverty, and death for others. There were some attempts among those whom society had cut off from any means by which to live, to organize themselves against this system that would, through neglect, destroy them. But their attempts were hopeless, and society became more and more split. . . . Somehow every issue they raised against the system was painted with some strange racial overtones. So as a result, none of the issues were ever dealt with. It was almost as if someone were sabotaging democratic activity purposely.

It was then that the people noticed the atmosphere: It was getting darker. With the darkness, for some, also came death. Some said it was some terrible fog that would sooner or later pass. Others said it was the chemical-spewing factories, which by now had replaced the filling stations in numbers. But the government quickly put an end to this talk. . . . Still others were led to believe that it was a poison-gas attack, the first wave of hostilities waged on one race by another. The mass media hysterically fanned the flames of racism as overpopulation was blamed for all the ills of the planet, particularly that of pollution, which was now obviously choking the world to death.

"Is there not a filthy element among us that pollutes not only our bodies and minds, but the entire planet?" The papers cried out.

Is not this element multiplying among us beyond all control? Something must be done!! And the establishment saw that it was.

RACE WAR

Dear Nancy

I've been holed up in Berkeley for the past few days, just hanging around the university and enjoying the weather. There is to Berkeley a kind of communal gestalt that I've never felt anywhere except Amsterdam—not even Cambridge. Berkeley is a student's city, filled with bicycles and old cars, lots of cheap places to eat and overpriced one-room flats. Parking is almost impossible, hustlers abound on Telegraph Avenue, just off campus. It being spring, it's almost time for the Berkeley municipal elections, and the radicals are out in force.

This year there's a chance, too, for something to really happen. A group of blacks, browns, displaced whites, and students have formed what's called the April Coalition, and they are running for all city offices, backed by much of the student community, and Berkeley's poor, too.

Poor because Berkeley isn't just another student community. It's bordered by Oakland, where some of the worst slums in the state exist, where the cops are legendary for being real pigs, and where the Black Panthers were born.

The April Coalition's platform, which was created last winter, has the support of most of the radical organizations in San Francisco and Berkeley. It's a good platform, too, including such matters as the restructuring of Berkeley's city government, community control of police, support for the Black Panther policy of self-determination and intercommunalism, women's liberation, a hard-hitting drug program to get heroin out of the Bay area, a referendum on marijuana—things that most thinking communities should implement now, but won't because the wrong people are in power. Here there is a chance—slight but nonetheless a chance—for some of the platform to be passed into law, if the April Coalition can organize itself by election time.

They've been getting help from a couple of guerrilla theaters in the area: the San Francisco Mime Troupe and a Berkeley conglomeration called the East Bay Sharks. If there is a theater that can pull together street people—the white kids who make up much of Berkeley's population—it is the Mime Troupe.

The Mime is, I think, the oldest performing guerrilla theater around, begun in 1959 by Ronnie Davis, who has since left. Presently, they run themselves as a commune, and are, in their own words, "dedicated to the overthrow of capitalism."

They are a strange mélange of people, the Mime. They live on something like thirty dollars a week each, in a number of communal houses, and work out of a headquarters on Alabama Street, in downtown San Francisco—an area filled with railroad trucks, warehouses, bums, and madly driven forty-foot trailer trucks.

The Mime is a theater basically of white dropouts. When Ronnie Davis started the Troupe, he was a dropout from the San Francisco Actor's Workshop, from which Jules Irving and Herb Blau moved on to such places as Lincoln Center. Davis moved into the streets, where he did Commedia-styled theater for anyone who would watch.

He collected about him other dropouts—notably Bill Graham, who got into the concert promotion because he produced some benefits in 1965 for the Mime Troupe, after he and Davis split up for what Graham calls ideological reasons.

At first, the theater was Commedia. But then, after the Troupe got arrested for what *Ramparts'* David Kolodney called "free entertainment in the public parks without a Ford Foundation grant," the form of their shows changed. Not really changed—but radicalized with the times. The clown costumes and minstrel shows like *Civil Rights in a Cracker Barrel* gave way to shows that dealt with immediate problems, like *Meter Maid*, which showed audiences how to insert aluminum tab tops into parking meters, or an ecology skit dealing with revolution as the natural course of events. Now, the Mime Troupe's repertory includes *An Independent Female,* an old-fashioned olio that I saw performed at the Ash Grove in Los Angeles, and *Telephone,* a guide to ripping off Ma Bell, for which *Ramparts* got sued when they published the script.

The Mime Troupe is not, by any means, a *nice* theater. More than any other guerrilla troupe—with the exception of, perhaps, the Buggerrilla—they are organized, know who their audiences are, and are fully—totally—committed to a revolutionary struggle against capitalism and the present Amerikan way.

There is a story: When *Meter Maid* was first performed, the Mime accompanied the play with anti-parking meter literature, as well as with a proposal for an alternative action, known, according to the Troupe's Joan Holden, as the "Aluminum Tab Top Strategy": those tear-shaped tabs that come on the top of beer and soft-drink cans are perfect to insert in parking meters, either serving as slugs, or rendering the meters totally inoperable. Then the Troupe demanded total and complete withdrawal of all parking meters from American streets, and the meters' recycling for better, more humanitarian uses.

In recent years, the Troupe has added puppet shows, "crankies" —a dramatic form that superimposes live action with a hand-cranked narrative (sort of a guerrilla theater with subtitles) and the Gorilla Marching Band—a Brechtian group of musicians who march and play at most all performances. There is also a rock 'n' roll band, Red Rock, that plays free concerts and benefits when needed.

Critics have not always dealt with the Mime in the kindest of terms, although they won an *Obie* in 1968, for—according to the citation—"uniting theater and revolution and grooving in the park." They have been arrested in San Francisco and, I guess, all over the country, for inciting people with their particular brand of theater. During one of their semi-annual tours in 1967 they were described by a mid-America critic as "irreverent, sacreligeous, lewd, suggestive, profane, vulgar, crass, and just plain dirty." It is a fitting description, too.

What is marvelous to watch about the Mime is the way they can do theater almost anywhere. I've seen them on stages, in the middle of crowds, in San Francisco's Union Square, at Provo Park in Berkeley (where they've been performing for the April Coalition), and rehearsing in their own Alabama Street warehouse. They perform with the practiced aplomb of old-time circus stars—which in a sense they are. And people who see them are impressed. Luis Valdez, remember, saw them at San Jose State when he was a student. When he left school, he joined the Mime. A lot of what the Teatro does was born on San Francisco streets.

More than anything else, the Mime is a beautiful consciousness-raising weapon. It presents free theater to people who are used to paying three, four, five, or six dollars for seats to some revival at one of the local theaters—and does it as well as any professional company in town could. Think of what it must be like for folks on their lunch hour to sit down with a sandwich and watch *An Inde-pendent Female* done while they eat. Especially male office workers, who can get really shook up with that particular play. And the Mime knows how to work, too, *with* an audience. They use cat-calls and booing, or cheering and whistling, incorporating it, im-provising around it, playing with it. In other words, they're good showmen. As Joan Holden said, "If somebody stands up and makes a comment, that's good. It means there's no distance between you and the audience; no walls. And that's the way it was meant to be."

Mainly, the Mime does theater that provokes people. It's not enough, they say, to have long hair, to listen to rock 'n' roll and groove. There has got to be positive action; each play has got to make a substantive suggestion for some kind of improvement, whether it's liberating women's consciousness (or men's conscious-ness about women), ripping off Ma Bell, or stuffing beer-can tops into parking meters.

Normally, the Mime is poor. They do one or two college tours a year, which gives them enough capital (pardon the expression) to get through another season of free shows in the parks. But they hate haggling over money with schools about their fees, which they're forced to do, because they dislike intensely what most schools do with "special funds."

"Look," said Jason Harris, "we go off to a college, and we're lucky to get fifteen hundred dollars. But the college puts like twenty-five grand aside for war research or ROTC recruiters or stuff like that. Or movies—movie rental. What a waste. But like all administrations, college administrations are interested in maintaining the status quo; and since we represent change, we're dangerous."

An interesting note concerning finances: In the early days, the Mime Troupe had relationships with most of the so-called revolu-tionary San Francisco groups: the Jefferson Airplane, the Grateful Dead, Quicksilver Messenger Service, and so on. All that has been dissolved now, mostly, I gather, because the Mime Troupe wants it that way. I can see their point.

The groups that have "made it" are ripping off the kids—who the Mime Troupe is focusing on these days—by charging six dollars a head at concerts. It's not a rip-off price, and it's not something that Bill Graham sets. But rock 'n' roll has become big business. So the Airplane sings "Up against the wall, mothafuckers," and they ride around in limousines. Or Bill Graham, who once worked for 120 dollars a month as the Mime Troupe's manager-producer-truck driver, now pulls down sixty or seventy grand a year as a promoter, and more from his related companies—publishing agency, etc.

That kind of thing, I gather, makes any further interaction between the Mime and the musicians impossible at the present, because the two groups see things in totally different ways. It's not as if the Mime is saying "power to the people" and not doing anything about it; it's just that they're dedicating themselves to something fully, and, I guess, can't see why other folks pay lip-service to the revolution while snorting cocaine in a limo.

The most recent play the Mime has put together is substantially different from their past work. Normally, the group works with comedy. It's easier because melodrama—the kind of stuff, say, Ibsen wrote, or Shaw—while entertaining to a "theater" audience, can't hold water on the street. On the streets it's got to be quick and dirty. Anyhow, the new piece is called *Seize the Time*, and it's a documentary play that deals with the Black Panthers—Bobby Seale and Erica Huggins, specifically. There are scenes from Bobby's book, from the Chicago conspiracy trial, and selections from conversations with Elaine Brown about Erica Huggins. Joan Mankin described the play as "a comment on reality. What we're trying to do," she said, "is tell the truth."

Much of the action is done in slow motion, and using masks. I hope that I have a chance to see the show, because it sounds interesting—both in content and technique.

I would also like to watch how the Mime works when they're *in camera*. They function collectively—like when I called and asked if I could come over and talk, I was told sure, but it would be to more than one person. Nobody makes decisions himself, or answers for the Troupe. It's all done in concert. Ah—one magnificent point: The Mime's phone number is suspiciously apocryphal: 431-1984. The last four digits are positively diabolical.

I'm enclosing a copy of *Telephone*, which is a really indicative work. The script really does look like a draft of something by Goldoni or one of those early playwrights, before complicated stage directions and what we call production values came into vogue. It's the kind of show that anybody could do—which is, too, what the Mime is all about. They're out to make people create their own theater and solve their own problems—a good thing to be doing.

Random note: Graffiti in the Mime's bathroom: "Does The Red Guard Dig Chinese Opera?"

More tomorrow from Berkeley, where the April Coalition is planning a street closing, and the East Bay Sharks are slated to perform.

Love,

j

TELEPHONE

CALLER *dials* OPERATOR.

OPERATOR: May I help you?

CALLER: Yes, operator, I'd like to place a long-distance call to Zap, North Dakota, station-to-station.

OPERATOR: Please deposit three dollars and ninety-five cents.

CALLER: Three dollars and ninety-five cents?

OPERATOR: Yes, sir, for the first three minutes, sir.

CALLER: But, operator, I'm calling my guru!

OPERATOR: Your guru, sir?

CALLER: Yes, operator, he's very sick. And I don't have that kind of change.

OPERATOR: Perhaps you could place the call from your home phone, sir.

CALLER: I don't have a "home phone, sir."

OPERATOR: Would you care to reverse the charges?

CALLER: That might kill him!

OPERATOR: Oh, sir, don't you have a credit card?

CALLER: A—credit card?

OPERATOR: Yes, sir. With a credit card you could place the call at your employer's expense.

CALLER: I could?

OPERATOR: Yes, sir. Suppose, for example, you worked for the Bank of America here in San Francisco. When the operator came on the line you would simply say, "Operator, I wish to make a credit card call. My credit card number is S-756-0400-158." And the call would go through without any further ado.

CALLER: What was that code again, operator?

OPERATOR: S as in Sabotage, 756-0400-158. (CALLER *opens coat, reveals that he is a* COP.)

COP: Thank you, and you are out of service.

OPERATOR: This is a recording?

COP: It's no use, Babs, we gotcha.

OPERATOR: But how? . . . How?

COP: We've had our eye on you for a long time, Babs—first it was just a bit of grass in the ladies' room on your breaks—now it's the big time, isn't it, Babs? The old story. Yeah, yeah, yeah.

OPERATOR: All right, I don't care, I hate Pacific Telephone! Why do they get away with being a monopoly? Why don't they lower their rates instead of printing all those glossy brochures to send out with the phone bills? Who for God's sake needs a Princess phone?

COP (*pulls gun on* OPERATOR): You're going to the Big House, Babs, for a long, long stretch.

OPERATOR (*gives* COP *karate chop and runs into audience*): Okay, everybody, the phone code goes like this: The credit cards are renewed annually, and S is the code for 1970. The second part can be any number in the San Francisco phone book. I just picked Bank of America because they're such a big company—they'll never notice a little extra padding on their phone bill. Did you know that more than ten thousand false credit card calls were charged last year to the Dow Chemical Company alone?

COP: All right, Babs, one more word and I'll blow your goddam head off.

OPERATOR: The last part, 158, is the city code of San Francisco. So the code is really S—any number in the San Francisco phone book —158. Always call from a pay phone—and always call station-to-station.

COP: All right, Babs, take that (*fires gun at* OPERATOR). These goddam M-16s.

OPERATOR: Because that way even if they catch on, there's nothing they can do—if the person you call is cool and just denies receiving the call. It's a bug in the system—and, brothers and sisters, they can afford it.

COP: Okay, Babs, it's all over. There's only one problem with your little scheme. Why take it out on the innocent public-spirited companies like Dow, United Fruit, Levi-Strauss?

OPERATOR: Because they're imperialist lackey running dogs and we should screw them whenever we get the chance!

COP: Hey, wait a minute, you're not gonna claim to be one of those political prisoners, are you?

OPERATOR: Sure, why not? In Cuba the phones are free. All of them!

COP: Okay, Babs, seeing as how you have all these weird opinions and all, we're going to have to throw the book at you. (*Takes out small book and throws it at* OPERATOR.) It'll be a swift and speedy trial, so let's pay a little call on the JUDGE-O-MAT.

OPERATOR: The what?

COP: The JUDGE-O-MAT—instant justice! The latest device in the war against crime and overcrowded courtrooms. Let's take a little mosey. (COP *and* OPERATOR *cross to puppet box where* JUDGE-O-MAT *appears.*)

JUDGE-O-MAT: Order in the court! Charge, please!

COP: Misdemeanor, your honor-mat.

JUDGE-O-MAT: Offense, please.

COP: Telephones, your honor-mat.

JUDGE-O-MAT: Oh, you must mean the old stamp dodge.

COP: The old stamp dodge, what's that?

JUDGE-O-MAT: The old stamp dodge—you know—not putting a six-cent stamp on your phone bill, so the phone company has to pay the postage.

COP: Oh no, it's worse than that, sir.

JUDGE-O-MAT: Then you mean the old spindle swindle.

COP: The old spindle swindle?

JUDGE-O-MAT: The old spindle swindle—that's punching an extra hole in your phone bill so the computers freak out.

COP: No, your honor-mat, this is credit cards.

JUDGE-O-MAT: Oh—you mean the old S—any number in the SF phone book—dodge.

OPERATOR: Hey—you're hip to the phone code—you musta been talking to some of my friends.

JUDGE-O-MAT: Felony! felony!

COP: No, no, it's a misdemeanor, your honor-mat.

JUDGE-O-MAT: Talking is conspiracy; conspiracy to commit a misdemeanor is a felony. Please deposit an additional ten cents. (MAN *does so.*) Sentence! Six months suspended, three weeks Santa Rita, one semester (*name of school*). Lock her up.

OPERATOR: Fascist scum, your days are numbered!

OPERATOR OF JUDGE PUPPET (*emerging barefaced*): Come on, lady, I'm just trying to do my job! (*To tune of "Yellow Submarine," dancing.*) Call your friends, it's just a dime/from California/on company time/say my cre-e-e-dit card is S/any nu-u-mber/158. (*In rhythm.*) You're under arrest.

BOTH (*dancing together chorus-line fashion*): Call your friends on the People's Telephone, People's Telephone, Call your friends (*etc.*). (*Dance off.*)*

* The phone company has changed the sequencing in credit cards. The 1970 code given is of historical interest only, and will not enable anyone to make illegal phone calls.

Dear Nancy

I sat for a couple of warm afternoon hours today in People's Park Annex, a lumpy two-block stretch of turf, rocks, improvised kids' toys, and picnic tables in the flats below the Berkeley Campus, while the April Coalition held a political rally. It was the first of two I went to, both within a space of four hours. At the first one there was beer, hot dogs, really great cole slaw, lots of kids playing around, and guerrilla theater, performed by the East Bay Sharks. At the second, there was only theater—the Sharks again, accompanied by a whole lot of handbills. The Mime was supposed to show up; they never did, although I saw a couple of people from the troupe in the crowd at rally No. 2.

The Sharks are a strange group. Four guys: Arthur Holden, Darryl Henriques, Phil Marsh, and Clive Flowers. All four live in Berkeley, and are what you'd call street people. But well-schooled ones. Holden has, I think, an M.A. in chemistry; the others weren't talking.

They make their money from what's collected when they pass the hat after a show—this afternoon, roughly twenty-seven dollars. Not bad from a small crowd. And they are, to say the least, a loose-knit bunch.

The Sharks have at first a very Brechtian feel to them. They gather people by unpacking a couple of the tiredest-looking suit-cases I've ever seen, filled with small props and instruments. Darryl plays snare drum, Phil sax and guitar, Arthur pulls out a cornet, and Clive pounds on a bass or puffs into a tuba. They stand in a line, looking like a George Grosz cartoon of Berlin Street musicians, and go into some of the most marvelously tacky riffs I've heard in a while. It's echoes of early Weill, combined with original lyrics and political overtones.

The Sharks wear no costumes—street clothes suffice—and limit the props to what they can carry in the suitcases, plus a couple of stools, and, of course, Clive's tuba. What makes them special is that they're beautifully versatile. For example, Darryl Henriques will, instead of saying "No!," say the line and then do a backflip. It adds to the excitement of it all.

For both performances, the Sharks did the same show—*The Incredible Adventures of Alice, or: Thimblewoman, Part I*—the complexity and lunacy of which is so unbelievable I will not try to explain it. Suffice it to say that it's a parable loosely based on everything from Spiderwoman comic strips to Alice in Wonderland to James Bond, with a few musical numbers thrown in for good measure, and a hefty dose of role-exchanging.

As a matter of fact, the closest thing I've seen to the Sharks is the Firesign Theater—which although they hardly ever perform, is a decent enough guerrilla theater in its own right, even though you can get the group only on LP albums or bootleg tape recordings. Both groups have the same kind of enforced zaniness—drawing on sources like the Marx Brothers or Spike Milligan's "Goon Show," instead of traditional theater—the Mime's use of commedia, for example, or the Buggerrilla's scripts.

Nothing seems to be written for the Sharks. They evolve their skits from improvisations, write the music and lyrics, but play around with the lines as the mood strikes. Which worked well this afternoon, especially in the second performance.

That one was held on the corner of Vine and Walnut, where authorities had closed the street to cars, and people gathered to hand out April Coalition pamphlets, eat organic food, and watch some street theater. There was a dance group made up of young kids, and a number of spectators who came in costume but didn't perform. But it was the Sharks and the promise of the Mime Troupe that brought out the 300 to 350 spectators to sit in the sun, eat food, and talk.

Funny thing I noticed: The crowd got very amiable after the Sharks performed. Perhaps because the Sharks elicit a lot of audience response. They're Berkeley's own street theater, and they act like unofficial city employees—reminding the folks to clean up after themselves, directing traffic—even talking with the audience during the show.

And unlike most of the theaters that I've seen, the Sharks have no real political message. There's an underlying dissatisfaction with the system in their play, but there are no solutions, except for the most generalized ones: Get yourself together, be natural, don't hurt anybody, keep on truckin'—the kind of flower-power stuff I heard back in 1967 from the Haight.

Yet they do a lot of politically motivated shows. If there is a benefit for prisoners, for an antiwar rally, for the April Coalition, the Sharks are there. If anything, they do reflect the attitude of laid-back radicalism I've seen around Berkeley for the past month or so —even with the election coming up. The stuff they do, with a drug culture, student, long-hair orientation, does well among street audiences in Berkeley.

And other places, too. I noticed, for example, in one of the "straight" Bay area papers last week, that the Sharks played at somebody's sweet-sixteen party—which makes them real mummers who'll play any gig if it pays the rent.

Compared with the Mime Troupe, the Sharks are weak—both philosophically and artistically. Their roots are about the same as the Mime's—displaced, basically middle-class white people who want, somehow, to radicalize the system. But unlike the Mime, which right out front dedicates itself to the overthrow of capitalism, which does shows to promote that goal, and which has organized itself to winning a revolution, the Sharks have no organization. Their artistic roots lie in comedy and music, surely social satire, but without any real philosophical basis. There is no overt goal to the Sharks' material—nothing concrete, that is.

But they're fun, and I thought you should know about them, because they're similar to a lot of other guerrilla theaters—with the desire to perform, a community to base in, and no real thrust to force change upon their community. I guess you could call the Sharks a consciousness-raising "force," rather than a straight political one.

Even so, they were somewhat of a disappointment. I kept thinking to myself: What a time Luis Valdez—or Ed Bereal—would have had if he had been a Shark.

One last note: When they pass the hat, the quartet goes through the crowd growling, "Feed a hungry shark. . . . Feed a hungry shark." It's very effective.

More soon.

Love,

j

east coast
letters

Cambridge, Massachusetts

Dear Nancy

Arrived in Boston three days ago, bused in from New York compliments of Continental Trailways, who had, would you believe, a stewardess on the express bus from New York.

It's been years since I was in Cambridge, but somehow I remembered how the MTA worked, and, without too much difficulty, made it from the Common to the Harvard Epworth Church, which is the headquarters for the Caravan Theater and a street theater, the Street Player's Union.

Cambridge is, well, Cambridge. You know. Old brick and white-painted wood. Lots of bikes, and green all around the Radcliffe yard. I walked for quite a time, having left all my luggage in New York, and watched people. Maybe that's what's best about Cambridge—the people-watching.

By the middle of the afternoon my feet were killing me and I decided to see if anybody at the Street Player's Union was rehearsing. It was Massachusetts hot and humid out, and the coolness of that old brick church was something I appreciated. I remember in California how I hated the hotness of, say, Madera, or the San Joaquin Valley. But it was dry heat. Hellish but bearable. Here, the sweat just pours off you.

Anyway, I was soaked to the skin when I walked into the church's basement, and found the SPU already rehearsing. There were seven of them, and they were putting together the show I ultimately saw two nights ago in Boston at a youth drug center at the Arlington Street Church, right off the Boston Common.

The SPU has been together about a year. Although they function collectively, making decisions as a group, the guy who did most of the talking is a young ex-New Yorker named Steve Seidel.

Originally, the group started out as an adjunct to the Caravan Theater, as a kind of experimental workshop that didn't need the permanent facilities that the Caravan has built into the Epworth Church: lightboards, bleacher seating, hanging drapes, and a few trunkloads of props.

But now it's a separate entity, performing where it chooses, and its members make their living, most of the time, from passing the hat after performances. They've even changed the name of the group—from the Caravan Street Theater to the Street Player's Union.

The thing I noticed most about the SPU is the way that they deal with life. They're basically white, middle-class kids who have been brought up within the system and for their own reasons chose to eschew it.

The theater that they do is basically emulative—there is nothing new in either form or content. The SPU's technique is a melange of acting-class styles and improvisation exercises, and the problems they deal with are those that can be read in any underground newspaper.

The feeling I get is this: Theaters like Concept and the Buggerrilla and the Teatro are fighting—literally—for their lives. Their audiences can immediately see the "why" for their existence. With theaters like the Sharks and the Mime Troupe and the SPU, the audiences—not street people, but the cats in the Boston Common, say—often can't really find a way to deal with the material the theater is presenting, because it's alien to them.

What I'm getting at is that instead of therapy for the audience, what the SPU is providing is therapy for the players.

Example: The troupe played at noon yesterday in the middle of the Boston Common. The audience was made up mostly of office and construction workers on their lunch hour, plus a lot of kids who were passing by. The SPU's reception was not good. Most of the people just didn't understand what the plays were all about. The theater began with a series of transference exercises—an old acting-class game in which one person starts a movement, and then another picks it up, organically changing it as he does so. Each member of the troupe does this, and when the thing has gone full circle, and gets back to the first person, he finalizes it by reverting to the initial movement. Now, that's fine for the classroom, but not many people on the street get what's going on at all. The funny thing was that the kids in the audience—which numbered roughly a thousand—got the point almost immediately, although the office workers catcalled and shouted jibes.

The SPU knows that they have problems with audience identification, too. They prefer to work with kids, simply because kids are more open to what they're doing.

And the plays that they do are really suited for younger audiences, too. There's a cat-and-mouse play that deals with role-playing, a women's play called *Smile,* and a dope play, all of which appeal to younger people—like the audience at the Arlington Street Church. There, amidst free vegetarian dinners that were supplied by volunteers, the audience really accepted what went on.

And the reason for that is with kids, the SPU is playing to equals. When they do a show for "straights," like out on the Common, there's no thread of identification. What hard-hat can get behind a play that deals with the role of women if he hasn't been inculcated with some background material?

The Teatro, say, can do plays about workers, and the Buggerrilla does a black women's piece. But those are issues that face Chicanos and black folks on a day-to-day basis. What the SPU hasn't done yet is really define their goals—decided what their theater really is all about. And who it's for.

They appeal to kids because kids can identify with the generalities that the group is talking about: role-playing, middle-class values, deodorants and feminine hygiene sprays and Handi-Wrap, ecology, pollution, sexism, drugs—those things. But the problem seems to be that the SPU isn't defining the issues well enough yet to be able to appeal to the audience they so much want to appeal to: that lunch-hour crowd on the Boston Common.

The reaction, as I said, was not kind. And in talking to cats in the audience, I found that people just couldn't see where a bunch of freaky kids were doing anything educational or provocative. People dug the tumbling and the running around—and a lot of the hard-hats really enjoyed the fact that the women in the theater weren't wearing bras. But things didn't go much farther than that.

The theater seems faced with a choice, then. Either it can perform for kids, and be accepted, but really not change anything because the audience (or 80 percent of it) already agrees with what the troupe is saying; or it can try to deal with the Boston Common crowd in terms that the crowd can understand and get behind. Now, I don't think that means doing hard-hat theater, or using conventional styles. Maybe what it means is that the SPU is going to have to look long and hard at their roots. What is the significance, anyway, of being a white, middle-class, dropout theater? What are the roots? Where is the theater coming from?

With the black theaters I've seen, the message is pretty universal: the theaters are talking about laying freedom on the audiences. And the Teatro is into cultural rebirth. Now I know that these are awfully generalized goals—you could argue that Sophocles was into laying both freedom *and* cultural rebirth on his audiences. But what I think I'm getting at is this: the minority theaters have a clearcut goal, toward which most of them seem to be proceeding both ideologically and artistically. Do the white guerrilla theaters have the same similarities as do black or bronce theaters?

They do, but there seems to be a lot more confusion within white theaters, a lot of hangups from "liberal" days, when talking about problems was equated with doing something about them. Also, the white population of America is much, much more fragmented than the minorities. If you're black, brown, yellow, or red, you stand out to begin with. You're made conscious—from the beginning—that you're "different." People who are "different" tend to stick together.

A lot of white people are just happy being what they are. They don't want to change or revolutionize anything. Others are typified by the Archie Bunker aesthetic. Still others just don't give a damn.

So white guerrilla theaters are faced with the problem both of trying to change things through theater, and of trying to unify an audience which is not only diversified, but wants to stay that way. The SPU has a real problem on its hands.

The motivation is there: they want to do theater, because they feel it's the best way of expressing the way they feel about what's happening in the world, what's wrong, and how to cure it.

Yet I have the feeling that what they're doing is too specialized if they really want, for example, to get to audiences of hard-hats in the Boston Common. Luis says that the Teatro has to keep ahead of the people—but only a step ahead, because any more, and the audience will lose touch with the teatro, and then it won't be a people's theater any more.

That could be the thing about the SPU—the theater might be too far in front of its audience to really get to them, to really change them.

In the Street Player's Union, for example, about half of the group has had "regular" theater experience. As they said to me last night, it's hard to disregard that background and adjust yourself to the necessities of guerrilla performance. People who are conscious of upstage and downstage, and tight form and content, and have learned not to improvise from the very start, are gonna have a harder time of it when they get out on the grass and somebody tosses a beer bottle in the middle of a scene, or a drunk wanders up and interrupts.

Also, in the very collectiveness of the theater there is a diversity that seems to me to be alarming. Sure, we all want the war stopped, and we want women to be able to shed their traditional roles if they want to, and we want to raise people's consciousness toward a better life and country. I'm not saying these things aren't important, 'cause they are. But it all seems so damned hard with a disenfranchised white theater to get those points across.

Jimmy Breslin once said that if you could get the hard-hats to go along with the long-haired kids, the war would be over in two weeks. He was right.

Arlo Guthrie says that people can't force change—that it'll happen only when the broad base of the population wants it. I don't agree. I think you can raise consciousness, and by doing that you can effect change. But how to raise the consciousness—that's the problem.

Like with kids: rock 'n' roll seems to have done it. Rock 'n' roll, as a matter of fact, is as good guerrilla theater as anything I've ever seen. But it's not an end. It's just something that, because it's exciting and loud, and the people who play it are attractive, people can get behind. If John Lennon has long hair, why shouldn't I have it too? If Mick Jagger smokes boo, why can't I? So people copy, and a whole new lifestyle evolves.

The problem that the SPU faces, then, is trying to synthesize the new lifestyle and values they want to promote, with some kind of valid confrontation between the audience and the actors.

That, according to Steve Seidel and the other members of the Street Player's Union, is what the whole magic of guerrilla theater is. "It's the magic of collective experience," he says.

"Look. Once you start doing street theater, and it becomes integrated into your life, you begin to see things. You look at events that go on and things that happen, and you see that you can make plays out of them. You try to take the things that concern you and express them to other people."

Seidel knows that the group has problems, though. He can't (and neither can anybody else in the group) pin the theater down ideologically. When I asked him where the SPU was coming from, for example, he said that it was "hard to say, because the plays we do don't have a revolutionary line or radical line or liberal line, so that it's hard to pinpoint an ideology or anything.

"More and more, though, we're realizing that we can't be just a theater group—that we have to connect with other groups that are doing antiwar or antidrug work, or with women's groups."

Dick Bloom, another of the SPU's members, added this, which I think is significant: "I think commitment is important," he said, "but the commitment has to be to each other—in the form of doing theater."

They also realize that they're going to have to focus what they do more. As Seidel said, "We're thinking about street theaters as community theaters more and more these days. If they really serve their communities, they can perform all sorts of functions: like go around and talk about social issues, or local things—like if a grocery store has been upping the prices, or the city hasn't put up a street lamp on a dangerous corner, you could do a piece on that. That's the whole function of a street theater—a living newspaper—just bringing issues into the community.

"Oh, it's a matter of entertaining people, but entertaining them with things that are real to them and immediate to them, and things that they can identify with."

Which, as I said to Steve, is all well and good. But what happens when the community is not a small section of a group of people—like the Teatro's audiences, but a whole city—like Cambridge, or, bigger yet—the whole Boston area.

His answer was that it's dangerous to identify with Cambridge because as a student community it's always changing. But the thing that the theater had to do was keep a large number of subjects available to play with. Diversity, Seidel felt, would keep the theater fluid and relevant.

It makes sense, I guess. But I'm still not satisfied with what the theater is doing. The Street Player's Union does know what it's talking about—and the plays they do are simple, decent street pieces. But I don't think they've focused themselves yet. I don't think that through diversity they're going to make people aware—really raise their consciousness.

Another example: I saw the Caravan Theater perform their play, *How to Make a Woman,* in Lexington last night. They're not a guerrilla troupe by any means, but an established theater that travels with sets, lights, props, and costumes. And yet their end result is as good as any people's troupe I've seen, because the Caravan has defined its audience, and is out to raise that audience's consciousness. For the past year, the theater has been exploring the man-woman relationship. The directors for the theater, Bobbi Ausubel and Stan Edelson, are a husband-and-wife team who have defined their own relationship in terms of the women's lib struggle. And as they worked out their own personal problems, the Caravan reflected their metamorphosis. Hence, *How to Make a Woman* deals with the myths and realities surrounding how, literally, women are made —in the physical, psychological, and sexual sense.

It's a play that goes from birth to death to birth. A series of commedia-like scenes, it is raw, opinionated, and highly evocative. Some things hurt—especially to men in the audience. Others are funny, some others as sexist as the male chauvinist pigs the play is talking about. But it's a good piece nonetheless: strong and dramatic, and done with flair. Mainly—and I don't care how much thought went into the production—the result of *How to Make a Woman* is that it hits you in the gut and causes you to look for some answers within yourself.

Another point: the most interesting thing about the evening was the after-performance workshop that went on.

The audience was divided into a number of groups segregating men and women, and, with the cast, discussed the play and what it meant to the people in terms of their own lives. The discussion was often bitter—I recall one German mathematics professor at MIT who hated the show. A divorced guy, his date had wanted to see it and he brought her not knowing that it was a women's lib play. All he wanted to do was take his date home and fuck her, and damn what she thought about him or anything. Now maybe he won't change, but his talking turned a lot of other heads around. And between the play and the discussion, I have the feeling a lot of people are going to see an immediate change in the way they treat their wives or the way their wives treat them.

I just hope that ultimately the Street Player's Union can do the same thing with *their* audiences—and that they can bring the kind of relevance they want out of the discussions they hold at rehearsal and onto the streets.

The SPU also gave me a script. Not only did they insist that I take it, but they signed a release that reads, in part, "We hope it will be performed all over, after people see it . . . and we don't care about copyright or money or any formalities. The play belongs to the people. (signed) Madeleine Winfield, Steve Seidel, Julie Rothstein, Lynn Lightfoot, Dick Kravitz, Richd. Bloom, Richard Baker."

More from New York soon.

Love,

j

INTRODUCTION TO
Women's Piece

Our women's play, or *Women's Piece,* which we call it, was put together when the women in the theater started swapping tales about the time when they were young and still living at home. We remembered the crazy things our mothers, fathers, teachers, and friends kept telling us about what we should be and how we should act. We found that we could bring back much of our experience with just a few words, like the ones in the piece, which say "everything," not just to us, but to an audience, too. After collecting the phrases we liked the best, the whole theater got together and put them into a pattern, using "Smile" and "You can never trust another woman," repeating consistently.

When we perform the piece, two women begin walking briskly in the performing space, stopping and turning abruptly—robotlike—whenever they make contact with each other or with a woman in the audience. One woman reads the script as she feels it, the others reacting freely to what she says. We usually find that it's helpful to maintain a rhythm with "Smile" and "You can never trust another woman." At some point toward the end of the script, the women begin to get angry, and gradually realize that they are each reacting with the same kind of anger, and that neither of them looks and acts like they are being told to look and act. They begin to come together and relate to each other more, while the woman with the script continues hurling more and more instructions at them, making up new instructions if she runs out of script. Finally, the other women protest—say that they're not going to listen any more, that it's all a lot of bullshit, and that she is free to join them if she wants. They insist that she join them, until she asks the audience if she should. Usually there's an answer to the affirmative. When that happens, she should throw her script in the air and join the other two women in a hug.

We encourage women to use our idea. However, you may find

it more exciting and fitting to start all over, collecting ideas and lines from your own lives, making up a whole new script.

The piece provides a good chance for people in the group to get to know each other, and hence the group's performance will be easier with friends, comrades in your memories.

POWER TO THE PLAYERS

The Street Player's Union
Cambridge, Massachusetts

SMILE

(*Women's Piece*)

Three WOMEN. *One with a script in her hands. The other two re-act robotlike to what she says. Playing to the audience, not to each other.*

WOMAN NO. 1: Smile.
Why can't you be ladylike, the way Suzie is?
Little girls don't fight.
Don't let the boys look up your dress.
Remember, you can never trust another woman.

(*All freeze.*)

Smile.

(*Other women smile. It is like a mannequin's grin—wide and toothy. Hold for a few seconds, then break on the next line.*)

WOMAN NO. 1: If you want boys to like you, don't do better than they do.

You don't need to say anything, just be a good listener.
You can never trust another woman.

(*All freeze.*)

Smile.

(*Same as last time. The grin, hold, and break on the line.*)

WOMAN NO. 1: Don't stand with all the other girls at the dance. Stand alone.

Why don't you have a date for Saturday night? All the other girls do.
Wait for *him* to make the first move.
Go out with anyone. It's good practice.
What kind of a girl are you, anyway?

You don't want to get a reputation like Suzie, do you?
Nice girls don't go too far.
It's up to you to stop them, because once *they* get excited *they* can't control themselves.
It's your fault if you get pregnant.
You can never trust another woman.

(*All freeze.*)

Smile.

(*Same as before. Grin, hold, and break on the line.*)

WOMAN No. 1: You can't trust a woman the way you can a man.
You can't afford to eat that—you have to keep your figure.
It's not good to be seen with such an unattractive girlfriend.
Smile.
Your new friend is too pretty—she'll take all the boys away from you.
Your eyes are your best feature, play them up.
Remember, you can never trust another woman.

(*All freeze.*)

Smile.

(*As before. Grin, hold, break on next line.*)

WOMAN No. 1 (*the pace is increasing*): Why don't you put on a dress?
Do something with your hair.
Stand up straight.
Put on some lipstick.
Smile.
Don't sit with your legs apart.
Hold your stomach in.
Smile.
Give yourself some color.
Smile.
Smile.
Smile.
Smile.

(*During this last section, the two women stop reacting like robots. They start to say No to WOMAN No. 1, and start acting naturally.*)

WOMEN NOS. 2 AND 3: Shut up. You know, you don't need to do that.

We're not going to listen to you any more.
Un-huh.
You know, we're beyond that kind of stuff. (*Ad-lib this kind of line.*)
Listen, why don't you stop all that crap and join us?
Really.
Join us.

WOMAN NO. 1: Naw. Naw.

WOMEN NOS. 2 AND 3: Come on. You don't really believe all that stuff, do you?
Join us.

WOMAN NO. 1 (*she looks at the audience for approval and waits until a woman in the audience says something affirmative*): Should I?
Should I?

   (*after affirmation*) Okay.
(*The three women embrace and exit.*)

Dear Nancy

I can remember when I used to catch the train from college into the city in the late spring, coming out of the greenery of the Hudson Valley and making that last fifteen-minute dash—down the Harlem River, across the 138th Street railroad bridge, and shooting down the tenement canyon that is Park Avenue above Ninety-sixth Street into the cool tunnel that runs south to Grand Central Station.

The houses that stretched from 138th Street to the entrance of the tunnel, on Ninety-seventh, were almost always lit up (I had the habit of coming into the city at night), and in the June heat, the people had moved bag and baggage onto fire escapes, ledges, and roofs to escape the wet New York heat at night.

As the train shot past windows, you could get a glimpse inside the tenements: pastel walls and clothes hung up to dry, and people hanging out of their windows, looking. Always looking. Sometimes there would be a street fair, with cheap rides and booths, set up on a blocked-off sidestreet. And there were always open fire hydrants, spraying kids with water.

But people never seemed to be doing anything—as if that tenement canyon were a place to just sit on the stoop and hang out. People with no bread just can't get out of the city to Fire Island, right?

When the Shakespeare Festival's Mobile Theater played Harlem and East Harlem in 1964 and 1965, I finally got out into those streets I had spent so much time riding past, and began to realize a little bit about what was going on there.

What I remember most are smells. Tropical fruit smells from snow-cone dealers, fresh watermelon smells, cooking smells from windows and restaurants, and poverty smells from stoops and alleys and yards. Poverty smells—it really does—and it smells the worst in New York for some reason. It's almost a tactile thing—something to be actually felt and tasted, even gagged upon, sometimes.

There were also sounds. Sirens—more sirens than in Detroit, which is a lot—and fire engines; and street vendors hawking everything from hot dogs to heroin. And the trains that run on the Penn-Central tracks on Park Avenue. Firecrackers, too. On July 4th one year, when we played a Shakespeare Festival performance of *A Midsummer Night's Dream* at 108th Street and Second Avenue, it sounded like World War II was going on outside our playground.

The neighborhood at 110th Street and Lexington is no different than most of East Harlem. The houses are old tenements, once owned by upper-middle-class Jews, now given over to blacks and Puerto Ricans—a change that started three or four decades ago and shows no signs of stopping. The basic word for this neighborhood is slum. Narcotics abound—I saw five dealers between the subway stop on the corner, and the community center where the Soul and Latin Theater, known locally as SALT, is headquartered. They lounged, three Puerto Ricans and two blacks, against cars in the garbage-filled streets and hit on passersby, asking if they wanted spoons or half spoons of Jones. On the corner, a vendor sold watermelons from the back of a truck. Two cops in a green-and-black bypassed the dealers, but hit on the melon man for some graft.

Three blocks west is the upper border of Central Park, where there is a boating lake, and where addicts like to sit on the grass and nod out. Little of the old culture remains here: an Orthodox Jewish temple on 107th Street and Fifth Avenue, Flower and Fifth Avenue Hospitals, and the New Lincoln private school, where you can send your kids and make them chic radicals—for about two grand a year, kindergarten through high school.

SALT is centered in a building that I can describe to you only as New York municipal. White brick-and-steel doors, it is covered outside with the gothic script of Puerto Rican street gangs, and its painted steel doors are etched with pungent and untranslatable graffiti. It's like a white-brick blockhouse, built by some occupying army as a safe location for the invaders to rest, out of contact with the streets, where they might get killed.

SALT shares the center with a number of other activities, most notably the Puerto Rican Dance Theater. As you go inside the building, there's a bulletin board, filled with posters made by pre-teen neighborhood kids—the same kind of poster-paint art you see at airports—and a heavy schedule of events: crafts classes, dance, and so forth.

I was early for SALT's rehearsal, but heard the sound of drumming coming from the gym, where the dance classes and basketball games are held, so I walked through a couple of sets of doors, and found a group—maybe fifteen or twenty—of teen-aged Puerto Rican girls doing classical ballet bar exercises to the beat of two conga drums and a set of bongos. I sat and watched fascinated while the kids, led by a tall black dancer, ran through a series of numbered positions and steps. Finally things broke up, and a community center technician began setting things up for the Soul and Latin.

SALT was founded in 1968 by Maryat Lee, a native Kentuckian whose first claim to fame was a play called *Dope*, written in 1950 or 1951. Currently she's trying to found a mobile theater in West Virginia with her associate, photographer-director Fran Bellin.

It all started when a group of young blacks and Puerto Ricans wanted to do a play about drug addiction, and a VISTA volunteer named Sandy Hoffman suggested that they get in touch with Maryat, who taught a course in street theater at the New School. What resulted was that Maryat coordinated the theater's activities and constructed scenarios such as *After the Fashion Show*, about homosexuality, *Day by Day*, a drug play, and *The Classroom*, a play about education. She didn't really write the words out, she said when I talked to her yesterday, but did outlines and watched while the kids improvised around them. Then she finalized the outlines, and the group performed them—keeping, however, the looseness of improvisation with them all the time.

SALT plays revolved—and still revolve—around ghetto themes: the neighborhood and its characters; the block. Like the Buggerrilla, SALT is out to show hustles—to lay freedom on the viewers. And like the Teatro, the problems SALT talks about in the shows don't go away at the final curtain or after the lights black out.

The people involved in SALT—the performers—are street kids, students at New York high schools who are learning about street theater, and about being urban guerrillas, by working together for ten weeks and doing shows on hot summer nights from the back of a flatbed truck. They have last names like Colon and Mojica and Braddock and Figueroa, and are sometimes known in the neighborhoods that the theater plays.

The troupe also includes a few professionals, but in nonperforming capacities. When Maryat Lee ran SALT, she was both the company's artistic director and their administrator. When Maryat began to feel that she was losing control by putting too much time in on paperwork, a young woman named Muriel Cherry took over the administrative duties. And last year a young black actor-director named Clay Stevenson replaced Maryat as artistic director.

Since Maryat's departure, the theater has started to change direction. They've recently moved into the community center from their old building, a warehouse on East 103rd Street, where there were no ceiling-high partitions and consequently very little privacy, along with a high monthly rent—something no street theater can afford.

But the change has been more than physical. The kids in SALT are third world kids, and the addition of a black administrator and black director has, I think, helped the company to focus on ghetto problems—on the problems faced by black and brown kids in New York—in a way that Maryat, regardless of how competent she is, could never have done. The kids respect Clay because he is a pro, but more than that, a black pro who can drop the cultured tones whenever he wants and rap with them in street terms. And he knows about the street as much as they, which is something they realize. Hence the results he's able to get are, I feel, more potent than Maryat's were.

Muriel is happy with the change. She's young, black, and interested in the community. And she feels that being in the center, despite its depressing architecture, is good for SALT, because the center is the only place in the neighborhood where kids can go to get a taste of the fine arts. It's also centrally located, which makes getting to rehearsals easier for SALT members.

She also talked about the goals of SALT as they exist. "It's theater for people who have no theater," she told me. "Look. This community can't afford traditional theater prices, and so they have no theater talking to them whatsoever. Hence theater has to go out to them, and it has to be theater that they can relate to. So what SALT does is deal with universal problems—but universal problems of the ghetto.

"The kids in the theater are street kids. They know about dope, and they know about dropping out of school, and what it's like to sit on a stoop because it's hot inside and nobody has any money to do anything. So that's what we do plays about, because that's what people in the New York ghetto are concerned with. Or maybe a play about getting out of the ghetto—how you do it. Anything like that can work.

"Like, last summer Clay wrote this piece about kids and what they do when they cut out of school—the problems that they face: dope, peer group acceptance, hustling—all of that. But he did it through improvs, and it made sense onstage—to the kids who acted it, and to the audiences, because the words Clay used were theirs. And we don't preach at the end, either. What we left the audience with was: 'Here's the problem. Your solution is just that—your solution. It's an individualized thing you've gotta work out for your own selves.'

"If you wanna analyze what we're doing, it's taking a ghetto situation that everybody knows, and visualizing it for people. It's like we're saying we've got to show you folks what's happening, and, you know, pick it apart for yourselves, and come up with some kind of solution, because we all know that the situation can't stay like it is."

SALT's season runs eight weeks, with five shows a week done on the end of their new flatbed truck. For the past few years, they've been operating off the end of a hay wagon, but it was easier, this year, to mobilize and be self-contained, rather than trust to towing the hay wagon around New York.

Unlike the Teatro or the Mime Troupe, SALT relies heavily on grants. Most of the street theaters in New York do, I found out, because it's hard to exist in their urban environment without government money.

Also, SALT needs the city, because they perform in the evenings, on closed-off blocks. They need the city to close the block, to give them power for microphones and lights, and to hand out whatever permits they need. New York urban guerrilla theater, it turns out, lives by New York rules.

Anyway, SALT was performing—an invited rehearsal, really—for a bunch of educators, as well as a group of coordinators from the Youth Services Agency of New York City, who will, in a couple of weeks, organize the blocks in which SALT will play this summer. The thing they're doing is called *The Block* and it's a classic kind of ghetto play—improvised around a chorus—that talks about sitting outside on tenement steps on a hot, muggy summer night.

Before the show, Clay Stevenson got the kids together backstage —the community center has one of those all-purpose auditorium stages—and talked to them. I guess it's something he does before every show.

Tall, thin—a dancer's figure, really—and theatrically flamboyant, Stevenson is respected by the kids because he is a pro. He's a Real

Actor and Director, who can relate to them both as performers and as street people.

"Remember—you gotta know what you're talking about," he said. "It's like we're at a disadvantage if we bullshit people, because we're on *their* block, and we weren't sent an engraved invitation to be there, you know?

"So if you bullshit them, and jive them, man, they're gonna jump up on your stage, and they're gonna act you right into the ground. They're gonna tear you A-Part!

"We all know the street, right?" A chorus of nods and yeas. "Well, man, the street is a test of where you are—of where your heads are at—so when we do the show, even for the cats out front in coats and ties, make it real. Show 'em where you are and where you're from."

The talk worked, I guess, because *The Block* is a real piece of theater—one of the realest I've seen in a while. It opens with a group of kids sitting on a stoop. That's the whole set—a stoop and a fire hydrant. The chorus goes: "Hot . . . damp . . . humid . . . mutha . . . muggy . . . fuckin'. . . ." Outside, the firecrackers started up. I could hear a train on Park Avenue, and the whistle of a jet, not so high overhead, on the LaGuardia flight pattern. Inside the center, it was really hot, and the educators and block organizers were beginning to sweat, just like the kids onstage, who had picked up a seven-way conversation about what to do.

One kid tries to hustle everybody so he can go down to the candy store and buy himself a soda. Somebody else does a mind trip on what it would be like to own an air-conditioned penthouse. Or a car.

"If I had a car, man," said a black cat, "I'd be baad. I mean, I'm mean with my own wheels, man. Like I'm my own man. I'd be free, if I just had the money. The bread, man."

Another kid: "I wanna get to the Bahamas, y'know? No cops, man. No pigs to hassle you. Just a lotta dope and broads."

There was a Puerto Rican chick in the play—she must have been like sixteen or seventeen. With the light on her, she looked like a Madonna. It killed me when she looked up and said, to no one in particular, "I wish, I really wish that I had something to wish for."

The play went on, and the fantasies came and went—in black ghetto slang and Spanish—a place with a clean bathroom, no rats, a two-story house in the suburbs, far away from the block and the stoop. Then all of a sudden things got hot.

"You make me sick," said the neighborhood militant. "All y'all do is sit on your asses and dream. It's all dreams, and shiit, it's all white dreams. Why ain't y'all dreamin' about freedom from the oppression of the white man? All I know about from living in this shit is hate, man, Hate."

Then all kinds of shit start to go down. Ideological arguments in street terms, fistfights—even a free-for-all dream sequence. And what people end up with after the twenty-minute play is a real sense of the conflicts that exist within the ghetto—all on the microcosm of that stoop. And what becomes obvious is that before anybody's gonna find a solution, people in the ghetto have got to get themselves together and organized. Otherwise, it's gonna be the same chorus over and over—every summer: "Hot . . . damp . . . hot . . . muggy . . . hot . . . humid . . . hot . . . mutha . . . hot . . . Fuckin' . . . hot . . . FUCKIN'!!!" And the lights go out—the kids are still sitting on the stoop, their heads folded in their arms, the sweat pouring off of them.

It works. *The Block* is a completely natural piece. The language is true, the actions have the same ease to them as any group of kids sitting on a stoop in the inner city. That was all proved to me later in the evening after the guests had left, when Clay put the troupe through a series of improvisations. Forced into a series of situations they didn't know about—playing fathers, mothers, and teachers—the kids were ill-at-ease and downright fretful onstage.

Sitting in SALT's crowded office later, Clay had this to say: "With the first play, the kids were able to work on it from the inside. They can accept the reality of the block—of the stoop—because they know it. Like when we started to work on the play, they knew that the whole thing started with the heat.

"Now, everybody down here in East Harlem can relate to their block in mid-August, you know, sitting on the stoop, when there ain't no breeze comin' from either direction. So therefore people—the actors and the audience—are going to relate, to identify with that. They're going to accept it and make it work—inside everybody's heads."

Something that grabbed me about the kids at SALT was their ease onstage—something, I found out, that Clay worked hard to give them. Unlike the stylized acting of the Campesinos, or the ghetto parodies of the Buggerrilla or Mime Troupe, SALT's kids are for real.

"Look, man," Clay said, "the thing about taking kids off the streets and putting them up on a wagon is that they've gotta know enough so that they can be truthful—and yet not so much that they're self-conscious and 'acting.'

"You take a kid off the street and put him on a stage, and he wants to *act,* and that's exactly what he's going to start doing—acting and orating—and that means he's not goin' to get involved. So what you've gotta do is get them to the point where they know they don't have to go through all those affectations they think acting is all about.

"That's when they start really cooking onstage."

Stevenson has spent a lot of time cutting SALT down to basics. Nobody ever gave him a course on theater in the streets, but instinctively he seems to have come up with a number of viable solutions for SALT and the neighborhoods that they play in. He's cut down on formal writing, letting the actors improvise as much as possible. And props, sets, and lights, too.

The result is surprisingly good in the street. I spoke to one cat who saw SALT a lot last summer, and he said that their major problem was trying to keep the audience from jumping onto the set and joining in. Everybody seemed to agree with what the actors were saying, and the number of "*Olés!*" and "Right ons!" was heavy.

Really, though, SALT seems to be headed in the right kind of direction. The problems of doing alternative theater in New York are immense. I was talking yesterday with Bobby Brannigan from City Center, who is trying to work out some kind of street theater program for this summer. Brannigan's a real good theater man—background as a stagehand, and at Lincoln Center for a long time, running operations there. But he has very little idea of exactly *what* alternative theater is all about, and how to go about doing it in New York. He has an idea he'd like to do a street and guerrilla theater festival this year or next, but doesn't know how many theaters there are, or where they can be found. There have got to be fifty or so in New York, most of them scrambling for funds from the New York State Council on the Arts. Many of them are in a constant state of flux—I tried to find Ed Faccini from the Gut Theater, a militant Puerto Rican guerrilla theater, with whom I worked at the Shakespeare Festival, but Faccini, and the Gut, seemed to have dropped totally out of sight.

It's a whole different world here in Gotham, I'll tell you that. Like I said before, this city has its own rules—even rules of guerrilla theater, it seems.

Tomorrow to Coney Island to see the City Street Theater. City Street is run by a couple of old radicals, Dick Levy and Marketa Kimbrell, and it'll be fascinating to me to find out if old-style radicals can do new-style theater.

Love,

j

Journal: Wednesday

Met with Dick Levy from the City Street Theater this afternoon. CST should be a change from the other theaters, according to the folks at the New York State Council on the Arts. It has no real neighborhood, but goes out on the road and performs in ghettos all over the country. Also, there's a small theater in Coney Island, where the company rehearses, and where they store their equipment and do occasional shows.

Levy, an off-Broadway actor, co-heads the company with Marketa Kimbrell, whom he met at Lincoln Center. Neither of them are kids, but I hear that the company is a young one.

Levy and I met at NYU, where he teaches, and walked down East Seventh Street to the West Village, where we stopped for coffee, on his way to the New School, where he is also teaching.

Impression: a pleasant enough guy. He has the New York off-Broadway actor feeling to him—competent but not brilliant; a man of considered actions without the vital energy of somebody like Luis Valdez or Ed Bereal. Maybe an academic at heart, I'm not sure. I do know, though, that he is a "head" cat, not a "gut" one. Maybe that's good—maybe that's what alternative theater in New York needs.

Then again, maybe not. I'm getting sick of looking through the *Village Voice* and seeing X number of experimental productions, all put together by people who have so-called bright ideas about theater. I would like, once in a while in this city, to see a show that's as effective to the gut *and* the head as the Teatro's *Soldado Raso,* or as maddening and provoking as the Mime Troupe's *Telephone.*

Maybe that idea is coming across, though, here in Gotham. When I talked to Bobby Brannigan, he said a couple of things that gave me hope—especially coming from an old China hand like himself: "The age of the entrepreneur's over. We don't need the Huroks any more, or the guys who call themselves heavy cultural experts. There's too much crap already on the boards—the best thing we can do now is get art to the people.

"Some guy says that art isn't for the guy who drinks beer. That's a lot of bullshit. The problem is that we've been so hung up bringing CULTURE to the people, we've almost blown it. Now's the time to get hold of some art—all kinds of art, too—that talks *to*, not *at* the audience. Or get the audience interested in getting its own art going."

Some heavy talking for a dude who cut his teeth on Broadway shows, and who had a hand in running Lincoln Center for a couple of years.

The question: Is City Street going to talk to or at the people? Best way to find out is to go, which I do as soon as they rehearse.

CST's history is promising: founded in 1967, when they produced some Lorca plays at Cooper Square Theater. CST is run by Levy and Marketa Kimbrell, both of whom have appeared with the rep company at Lincoln Center, neither in featured roles. The theater went to Washington in 1968 to Resurrection City in Washington, where they performed poetry and Lorca. Then the CST moved onto the streets, where it performed in New York during the summers of 1968 and 1969. Summer 1970 was spent touring the United States and playing to poor (i.e., ghetto) audiences in such places as Oakland, Detroit, Chicago, West Virginia, Delano, etc.

The question I have, though, is whether a theater can play to everybody—blacks, bronces, poor whites—and still keep a focus. Just whom is the therapy for—the audiences or the theater? Whom does the CST serve?

Will find out soon.

Journal: Thursday

The City Street Theater is more like a small theater group than any of the other theaters I've seen so far. Very much concerned with the aesthetics of what they do; very wrapped up in a kind of social theory that makes them take their theater, and themselves, seriously—perhaps too seriously. I'm still not sure at all how effective they are—whether or not they're as effective as, say, the Shakespeare Festival's Mobile Theater, or the University of Southern California's Theater in the Streets.

The theater is in Coney Island, at the end of the subway line, at Stillwell Avenue. You get off, wander over to Nathan's Famous to buy a hot dog and some fries, and head out to the theater, a block away. CST got their present building from Nathan's. A gaily painted storefront outside, and inside deep earth tones, revolutionary posters on the walls, and props and masks hung up display fashion.

Despite the rules on the wall, Marketa and Richard are in full artistic control, or so it seems. Presently the theater's working on the summer program, an adaptation of Gorki's *The Mother,* combined with *The Stations of the Cross,* a series of tableaux.

The company numbers seven—mostly young people. One couple, Peter and Maggie, went to Cuba last year with the Venceneramos Brigade. Peter met Marketa and Richard when the CST played Oakland, where he was living at the time. Of all the people at CST, he and Maggie seem to be the most committed ideologically.

Money comes from grants. Unlike a lot of theaters, CST is willing to take anything it can get, so long as the grant doesn't stifle them artistically. Richard said to me: "We don't consider that the money we get is really government money. After all, it really comes from the people, and if we left it with the government, what would it be used for? Only if they said to us, 'You can't do this or that,' or tried to censor us, would we stop taking it."

The style of CST's productions seems to have evolved out of the exercises that they do. There are warmups—ballet exercises, and sense memories, and transference stuff—all the things that take place in basic acting classes. Reason: Both Richard and Marketa teach, or have taught, acting. The company verbalizes almost everything, analysis being a big part of what they do.

I asked Marketa about the reasons for doing the type of plays that CST performs (last summer it was *The Bremen Town Musicians;* this summer the Gorki). Seems to me that by performing such generalized stuff, they can't hit at anything specific—especially if the theater is committed, as she and Richard say it is, to the overthrow of capitalism.

Marketa: "We don't feel that we can go into a neighborhood and tell the people how to live. But we do feel strongly that in this country the real problem is that people are alienated from their own groups. They have no dignity. The poor have bought that whole thing that's taught to them on television—that if you don't own, you're shit.

"You don't go to these people and say do this or do that, but provide them with a voice which comes from their own lives—from their own dignity.

"We had this guy with us—a real revolutionary—who played the preacher in one of the shows last summer. We were playing to an audience, and all of a sudden he got up and made fun of God in front of them, and some of them got up and left. We should have sent him away after that: To throw mud at people's values is to make them feel ugly.

"Political theater can be so specialized in its ideas that you end up condemning people through the ideas you promote. We stay away from that by choosing folklore that has a deep association with people's daily lives, and then we select things that connect them to their roots."

I asked how this works, thinking back to the Teatro's use of signs in the actos, and the simple statements they make: To show downtrodden workers, a dude wearing the sign PATRÓN stands on the backs of two ragtag-clothed cats who wear signs that say CAMPESINO.

The reply didn't quite satisfy me. Marketa said that as the theater's aims are socialist—their convictions being ones of "compulsively sharing the goods"—it's important to show that even though, say, mine owners are bad cats, ultimately it's the system that makes them so. CST, then, is concerned with identifying the enemy.

But the question is: Does *Bremen Town Musicians* do this when the images are artistically hidden behind folktales? Isn't the Buggerrilla's *Uncle Sam* more effective, because with that play, you see the game—you see that Sam is doing his thing to the pigs as much as he's running it on the niggers?

Originally, CST dealt with urban problems—like the improvs in their booklet. But now they seem to have gotten away from that and deal with—what? I'm not sure I know at all.

When I read the CST's account of their 1970 trip, which they hope to publish, I was amazed at the number of bad reactions they got—by their own admission. In Oakland, Peter got beaten up. Even in Coney Island, they had a hard time drawing an audience.

Richard said something, too, that shocked the shit out of me. He said that CST had given up on Coney Island, because it was impossible to play to an audience there. Maybe the reason is that for all their good intentions, CST are a group of outsiders, who don't live in the community, whose roots are not part of Coney Island's, now that it is a Puerto Rican slum neighborhood. Maybe their roots are elsewhere—both ideologically and artistically.

The motives are pure, but the implementation doesn't seem to be working. I watched a rehearsal; watched it unfold. The direction was all Richard and Marketa. They provided the artistic choices. Yet the rules on the wall say that everything is shared. I have no doubt that what results from the exercises—from the Penderecki "Passion and Death of Our Lord Jesus Christ According to Saint Luke" that they're using for background music, will be affective artistically. The thing I question is to whom it is gonna speak.

Next door to the CST is the New York branch of Peter Schumann's Bread and Puppet Theater. The basic excitement generated by ten-foot-high puppets has a lot more instant appeal than a troupe playing Gorki's *The Mother*. So does the Buggerrilla's *Uncle Sam*—just because the audience can grasp the game as soon as the characters appear.

To whom does intellectual guerrilla theater appeal? That seems to be the question.

"Our aims are purely artistic" is what Marketa said to me. I believe that.

I don't think I'm being elitist, either. The Free Southern Theater has done "difficult" plays for audiences unaccustomed to seeing theater, and people who've worked with them say it's been effective. So it's not necessary to do only living comic books, or actos, with first-grade-level plots. Maybe what I'm saying is that the CST is still finding itself as a theater. The intellectualizing is past for the Teatro because the goals are clear. In CST's case, things are a lot less clear.

There are the problems, for example, of two actors with radical backgrounds and twenty or so years of experience between them, dealing with kids who have never acted before, or who have only worked in college plays. This makes for a lot of coaching and spelling out. But if that's the case, what about SALT? Why do the kids in SALT do so well on an instinctive level, while CST's people seem to founder about? Not being elitist, I think, but practical. Or perhaps the first thought was right: that CST isn't a street theater at all, but a theater group—Caravan Theater comes to mind, or one of the experimental things at Judson Church, or Center Theater Group's New Theater for Now—that should do off-off-Broadway stuff in a small house in Soho.

All I know is that I feel that something's missing from CST— some kind of a spark that I saw elsewhere in the country.

SIGN ON THE WALL AT CITY STREET THEATER

The City Street Theater stands for active personal interaction and struggle because it is the weapon for insuring unity within the company and for maintaining the vital connections with the needs and struggles of the people.

We need to understand that LIBERALISM rejects this struggle and stands for unprincipled "peace," thus giving rise to self-indulgent and derisive attitudes that bring political and artistic degeneration.

Liberalism manifests itself in various ways:

1. To let things slide for the sake of peace and friendship when a person has clearly gone wrong and refrain from principled argument because they are an old friend, a loved one, a fellow townsman, a colleague, or a subordinate. Or, to touch on the matter lightly instead of going into it thoroughly, so as to keep on good terms. The result is that both the company and the individual are harmed.

2. To indulge in irresponsible criticism in private instead of actively putting forward one's suggestion to the company. To say nothing to people's faces but to gossip behind their backs or to say nothing at the meeting but to gossip afterwards. To show no regard for the needs of other people or the company but to follow one's own inclination.

3. To let things drift if they do not affect one personally; to say as little as possible while knowing perfectly well what is wrong. To avoid risk and be worldly wise and safe without blame.

4. Not to follow the express collective desires of the company but to give pride of place to one's own opinions. To demand special consideration from the company but to reject its discipline.

5. To indulge in personal attacks, pick quarrels, vent personal spite or revenge instead of remaining vulnerable and struggling against incorrect views.

6. To work half-heartedly without a definite plan or direction. To work perfunctorily and muddle along. "So long as one remains a monk, one goes on tolling the bell."

7. To regard one's self as having rendered great service to the company, to pride one's self in being a "old hand"; to disdain minor chores while being unequal to major tasks. To be slipshod in work and slack in study.

8. To be aware of one's own mistakes and yet to make no attempt to correct them. To refuse to accept others' feelings as a reflection of yourself. To take a "liberal" attitude toward one's self.

9. "An actor must be ready to join the creative act at the exact moment determined by the group. In this respect his health, physical condition, and all his private affairs cease to be his own concern. . . . We must not go short on sleep and then come to work tired or with a hangover. We must not come unable to concentrate. The rule here is not just one's compulsory presence in the place of work but physical readiness to create."

JERRY GROTOWSKI

10. No drugs or alcohol in the theater. Avoid lateness. Call in case of emergency.

11. Participate in the physical chores of the theater. Do not allow yourself to exploit and live on the labors of others.

12. Rehearsals are private.

13. Problems concerning work and other matters are not to be raised during work sessions. Rather, bring them up after work or at breaks and at regular discussions.

THREE IMPROVISATIONS

THE CITY STREET THEATER

HOW THE WEST WAS WON

An American pioneer, in quest for property, tries to get an Indian chief to let him invest in his land, promising the Indian a share in the profits.

The Indian is wary of the deal and claims that the land already feeds all his people.

The pioneer says that the chief has no right to deprive his people of the additional profit to be made by his investment, and he proposes elections enabling the people to make their own choice.

The chief explains that it is not the custom to have pioneer-style elections, and as far as profit goes, experience has taught his people not to expect much in dealing with the white man.

The pioneer, pushing the Indian aside, starts unloading his surveying equipment, at which point the Indian sees no other alternative but a fight.

In the midst of the battle (with garbage can lids and sticks) the pioneer loses his weapon. The Indian immediately stops fighting, explaining that, in the custom of his people, one never attacks an unarmed opponent.

The Indian turns to pick up the pioneer's weapon and is immediately stabbed in the back.

The pioneer stands over the body of the Indian chief and sings, "This land is mine, God gave this land to me."

HELP! I'M IN THE HOSPITAL

A woman in the last stages of labor seeks admission to a hospital. She is confronted by a nurse equipped with extra-large admission forms, who detains her with questions—previous illnesses of nearest relatives, the nature of her disease, subversive organizations she has belonged to, etc.

While the nurse proceeds mercilessly, the woman lies down on the floor and begins to deliver her baby herself.

A research doctor, attracted by the woman's screams, enters and begins to do research on the woman, inspecting her teeth, etc., but not offering assistance with the birth.

The infant begins to arrive as the nurse, having learned that the woman is on welfare, is demanding a deposit.

The doctor snatches up the newborn child, informing the woman that this operation will cost her nothing if he can use her baby for a little experiment.

When the woman protests, the doctor jabs a long needle into her arm, and, as she passes out, he informs her that she, too, has just been dedicated to research.

With the baby under his arm, he goes off, telling the nurse, who is still asking questions, not to let anyone disturb him; he'll be in the laboratory.

MOVING DAY

In front of a newly built high-riser. Covered with an odd assortment of blankets and coats, a group of people sleeping. Nearby on the sidewalk lie boxes of their belongings and a hot plate plugged into a lamppost.

The people awaken to the day they have all been waiting for. Having camped on this ground for eight months since the time their slum houses were torn down to make way for the new structure, they are now ready to move into the just-completed building.

They prepare for their last morning in the streets, sending the youngest kid out to steal, for the last time, the daily bottle of milk, carton of eggs, and newspaper. Toilet paper in hand, Granny, taking Rocky the dog with her, charges out for her morning mission, wishing herself success and solitude. Blankets are folded and the coffee put up for the last outdoor breakfast.

Just then the guard assigned to begin duty at the new building comes on and tries to get to the entrance by pushing away boxes, frying pans, etc.

The people begin to plead and argue with the guard, but they stop short to cheer as Granny returns with a very small roll of toilet paper, mission successfully accomplished.

Granny reads aloud from her diary the story of the eviction.

Discovering that these people actually intend to move into the building, the guard checks the list of expected tenants. They are not listed.

The people are aghast at the possibility that they will not be able to move in. They explain how, before their houses were torn down, they were told they'd be the first to get space in the new building.

That may be, explains the guard, but since that time the building, originally designated as low-income housing, has been changed to a middle-income project, and they can only qualify by proving a steady and appropriate income.

No one has a job except Granny, who earns very little as a fortune teller.

A black worker in the group, Max, explains that he begged for days to be given a job on the construction of this high-riser, but was refused and finally threatened. The guard tells him that another building is about to go up across the street and that he should go straight to the contractor if he really wants a job.

The people dress Max up, hanging a tie and their hopes on him, and send him out to see the contractor.

Max approaches a window marked by a sign reading, "CONTRACTOR." A man wearing a white hood appears. In answer to Max's request for a job on the construction site, the hooded man explains that the union is getting a little stubborn on this matter and that, while things are getting better after all, one can't rush such issues, this being a free country. Certainly City Hall seems to have solutions to all these problems.

Max walks to City Hall, where the same hooded man appears at the window. This time he tells Max about the Administration's new austerity measures, designed to improve things by making the rich much richer in the expectation that their wealth will trickle down to the poor. Unfortunately, right now there seems to be a snag in the trickle. But these are community problems, and the Chamber of Commerce has been doing miracles with their investments into communities. Certainly they should be able to help Max.

Buoyed by all the attention he has been getting, Max appears at the window marked "CHAMBER OF COMMERCE." This time, the hooded man, leaning out, does not even see him, but merely remarks on how black it looks outside. And he shuts the window.

Max wanders back to the street home and his family. Sadly, but with a spark of hope, they all move to the sidewalk across the street, where, eight months from now, another high-riser will be ready.

END

motown theater concept

Dear Nancy

I am in Detroit and I am afraid.

It is three in the morning, and I am sitting in the main office on the second floor of Concept East Theater, a turn-of-the-century stone building just off Woodward Avenue, Detroit's main drag, which runs from the Canadian border tunnel downtown, out north to Pontiac, where the Ku Klux Klan is still active.

I am sitting here with a soul station playing on the portable radio that Len Smith, Concept's director, lent me, this typewriter, some paper, and a shotgun.

Outside it is cold and drizzling. Through the rainy mist, I can see the Fisher Building, where the town's only major commercial theater is located, and the General Motors Building, its five-foot-high red neon letters burning into the blackness.

I have the shotgun because Paul Davis, Concept's technical director, thought it would be a good idea to have some kind of protection. The theater is housed in an old Catholic high school, has forty-two classrooms, and has been plagued recently by vandals. The burglar alarms aren't working, and the doors can be kicked in easily. What Paul told me was: "We'll be back at like six in the morning. Lock yourself in the office, and be cool. But if somebody comes in before six, it ain't gonna be us, and your face might get them uneasy or mad or both."

I called Larry DeVine at the *Free Press* today, and made an appointment to see him just before I leave Detroit. He assigned me a freelance piece about Concept—which is great.

The city on first sight is a racist company town. During the day, downtown is filled with middle-class white people, who all flee at 5 P.M. After that, the core of Detroit is left to its black majority—and the derelicts, the smackheads, the whores and pimps, and the poor. "Party stores" that sell booze, patent medicine, religious candles, and dream books clog the ghetto. Most run by whites. Some have armed guards, others rifle portholes behind and over the counter, where an employee waits with a 30.06 or an M-1, ready for action.

The money is all elsewhere. Either in heroin—130 people were

killed here last year in the so-called "heroin wars," reputedly in-
stigated by a guy named Marzette, a black ex-cop known as Detroit's dope czar—or in big business. But nothing is put back into the
city—downtown—at all. Oh, there's a civic center: Cobo Hall and
Convention Arena and Ford Auditorium, both on the river. But
on the community level, no place for people without the price of
admission to go. And little organizing in the community to remedy
that.

That's where Concept hopes to come in.

I sat, this afternoon, with Len Smith—Smitty—and Paul Davis in
a black bar on John R. (Actually, I shouldn't call it a black bar—all
the bars on John R. are "black" bars.) We talked about the kind of
theater Concept is growing into. It used to be a small house—fifty
seats or so—on Adams, which is right downtown on Detroit's skid
row. But the Archdiocese of Detroit was talked—Smitty says conned
—into giving the theater the old Salesian High School last winter.
What Concept wants to do there is create something Detroit's never
had before—a real black community theater center.

"It's gotta be a people's theater," Smitty said. And the logo of
Concept—"FOR THE PEOPLE"—conveys that intention. But because of the unique situation in Detroit, Concept is going to be a
different kind of people's theater than any other in the country.

First of all, Smitty has a real monkey on his back. A forty-two-
room high school is a lot harder to keep going than the box of
theatrical props that Ed Bereal can store for the Bodacious Buggerrilla in his apartment. The building is also in wretched shape, and
it's gonna take a lot of cleaning up and refurbishing before it starts
to even look decent.

Perhaps the deeper problem is the mood of the city. After the
1967 riots, the cops have become most repressive in their treatment
of black brothers. The municipal authorities said that the riot area
would be cleaned up and that there would be urban renewal, but
when we drove through last night, much of it still looked like
Dresden after the fire-bombing. And with the blue-and-white police cars prowling the dark streets, the inner ghetto of Detroit more
resembles an occupied country than a supposedly free city. Sure
there are a few programs—but they're mere trickles.

What's lacking in Detroit's black community is any deep "let's
get it together" movement. The dope is peddled by black pushers.
Some of the most dangerous and brutal cops on the force are black

—and today somebody told me that a few of the cops are known —widely—as paid, hired killers for the heroin dealers.

With no feeling of community, the black brothers in Detroit are being literally skinned alive. First by their own folks, and then by the Grosse Pointe and Bloomfield Hills crowd—who control the business—and the money flow—in this city.

It shows in the ghetto streets. Half-ripped down houses with people living in them. Boarded homes, condemned by the city but left standing, where addicts live. Gangs of street kids moving like wolfpacks down alleys, looking for somebody to roll.

Here in Detroit, people—black people—have an almost indescribable aura about them. Lots of sharp street clothes—jumpsuits, knits, poorboy hats. Cadillacs are big, too, and Buick Electra 225s. But on the street, there's an undercurrent of bitterness; a subcutaneous mood of hate and fear that can literally be smelled.

Hence the shotgun. And this city has affected me so much in the forty-eight hours I've spent here that I'm not at all sure I wouldn't pull the trigger if someone came through that door right now.

The rawness, the bitterness of Detroit is reflected in the city's music and counterculture. This is where—or at least in Ann Arbor, forty-five miles away—SDS was started. It's where John Sinclair, now in jail, founded the White Panther Party.

The music is rough, too. Mitch Ryder and the Detroit Wheels; the MC-5 and "Kick Out the Jams, Mutherfuckers." There is no subtlety to this place.

So what of theater here? What of Concept?

In two days I've come to a few conclusions. Smitty is a good cat. He's got a bad (in the good sense) head. A ghetto kid who knows where his roots are. Young (he's twenty-eight) and vital, he's trying to cope with running a theater that would cause the administrators at Lincoln Center to blanch. Almost single-handedly he's working to create three theaters in a decrepit old building whose pipes are burst, whose floors buckle eight inches in some places, and whose boiler is completely kaput. All this with no bread. And at the same time he's earning a living by teaching black theater at Wayne State University.

Now that's a story. Last year the people at Concept got together and picketed Wayne, because there was no black theater being done. Wayne's philosophy, you know, was the same old story about how actors should be able to do Shakespeare no matter what color they are. Well, that's true to an extent. But not when your roots are denied you, which is what was happening at Wayne. Concept did a flyer, which I'll enclose, and picketed. At first there were some really bad vibes between the Concept folks and some of the black students, who considered Smitty's people outsiders. But Smitty won out in the end, because finally, Wayne had no choice but to accept the obvious: If you're a school located in the middle of a ghetto, sooner or later you gotta get involved on one level or another with the community. Now, what's happened is that a lot of Concept's people are at Wayne, and folks like Smitty are teaching and directing there.

Smitty has what I consider a righteous attitude toward theater. He sees it as a mover of society. "Bring it in off the stoop and let people see life," he told me today. "Deal with the problems we face on a day-to-day level in Detroit, and provide answers for folks —theatrically—and you're beginning to do something.

"Now, the question is, how we gonna do that? Well, one answer is that Concept is out to change the attitude toward theater that blacks have. It's always been—like in the early days when Ameer Baraka was doing *Dutchman* and the like, 'kill whitey, kill whitey, kill whitey.' Fuck whitey, man. I ain't got no time to worry 'bout whitey. I gotta get the brothers together first. Then we can see what kind of relationship we want with whitey."

So what it becomes is self-realization. Laying freedom on people —giving them a sense of historicity, of their roots. Showing the problems and providing some solutions. Nothing out of line, but a step at a time.

Like doing improvisations about Detroit. Or plays by young black Detroit writers who need to see their words brought to life.

And equally important, working with young kids. The importance of drama workshops for young kids is unmistakable. Like Black Panther Free Breakfast Programs, a dramatic workshop can start a kid really thinking about just who he is and what his relationship is to the world in which he lives.

Or giving kids material that deals with the day-to-day problems of Detroit. Better yet, letting them create their own material. What does a ten-year-old think about the pimps on his block? Or the smack dealers? How do you break through the antihero worship that street kids have for incredibly evil people? And they do: Malcolm X was a Detroit Street kid when he went sour. As he wrote, he—and millions more—didn't have any alternatives.

What is there, after all, in Detroit now? Nothing, really. The church, school, the movies. Food is Pepsi and potato chips.

Who tells kids what's cool or uncool? They see it on the street corner. The pimp with the Caddie is cool; the pigs are uncool. Straight people are uncool. So is school. What's the future? Chrysler? Ford? General Motors? Smack?

It's a circular syllogism. Sure, you say, educate. But relevant education is nonexistent. The Detroit schools are eighty million dollars in debt. And with the community so goddamn polarized, there's no way to go.

Theater may be an answer. Not the best one, but an alternative to nothing. It's also palatable—exciting—and ostensibly it's easy to do.

It can also, pardon the expression, say sooth. Like the Buggerrilla does, it can make laughable objects of the liars and con men— on the street and in the government. It can take economic and social issues and deal with them in simple terms. In a few words, it can lay freedom on people, whether they think they want it or not.

I think that's why Smitty wants a large, not a small people's theater. Detroit needs a focal point now more than anything else. Sure, performing in the streets is important. But what's equally important here is a place that people know is constantly available to them.

If he can hold out, I think Concept will become a real viable force in Detroit. But there's got to be a lot of hustle first. He has to prove to the community that he's trustworthy, not another ghetto ripoff.

Right now, fear is prevalent. People don't trust people. Smitty's an exception. I got here with no place to stay, and very little bread. He put me up at the theater, opened all the files, and said, "Look through and take out and copy anything you want."

Sitting here now, the radio on and Bobby Womack blasting in the poster-filled office, the shotgun across the desk, I am strangely at home. Afraid, but at home.

There is a strange attraction that Detroit has. I've felt it even in these first two days. Love-hate. *Yin-yang.* Whatever.

Of all the theaters I've seen so far, Concept has the longest way to go. That's because Smitty has the love-hate thing for Detroit, too. He's been around, and he knows what he's up against. But Concept also has the most potential of the theaters I've seen, too.

Maybe that's because they've got the biggest neighborhood: the whole of central Detroit.

Tomorrow we do more painting here—I've been working, too— and then some people to talk to. The next three days are more of the same.

Love,

j

CONCEPT EAST PIECE

BY JOHN WEISMAN

Wire Press Rate Collect to Larry DeVine, Entertainment Ed., Detroit *Free Press*, Detroit 48231.

BLACK PEOPLE DON'T HAVE TIME TO GET TIRED—
KEEP ON PUSHIN'!!!!!!!
> *Concept East General Meeting Notes*
> *Spring 1971*

"I've always felt that black theater should deal more and more with community problems," says Leonard Smith, the energetic young, revolutionary executive director of Concept East. "We've come a long way from the old plays like *Dutchman* and *We Own the Night,* where the message was 'kill whitey, kill whitey, kill whitey.'

"We're at a point in our development where black people have got to stop treating white people as the focal point of their lives. We have our own problems and our own culture. There's no need any more to be so preoccupied with whites.

"Black art in general and black theater in particular has got to deal with black life—our roots, our heritage, our essence. And the only way it can do that is to start on a gut level—here in the community, where the brothers are."

Smith's theatrical philosophy is being implemented these days at the old Salesian High School on East Harper, where Concept makes its home. The school, built in 1914, was abandoned two years ago by the Archdiocese and remained empty until this past January, when the church leased the vandalized, ice-coated building on a rent-free basis to Concept.

The parochial influence, although diminished, is still visible. Rosettes are worked into lath moldings. The faded image of a crucifix hovers high on some walls. Floors are warped, the result of burst pipes this past winter. Ceilings with peeling plaster are not uncommon. But the four-story building, with forty-two classrooms, a gym, cafeteria, and offices, is being resurrected by Concept as a focal center for the black arts in Detroit. This week, the official opening takes place with a seven-day Black Arts Festival that will include theater, dance, art, and literature.

To get the theater ready in time for the festival, volunteer crews have been working overtime, painting the gym and surrounding rooms, and loading in the platforms and supplies necessary to build a theater-in-the-round for Concept's shows. Even Len Smith, a paper bag serving as a makeshift painter's cap, finds time to work.

"This place is a godsend after our last theater, no matter how dilapidated it was when we moved in," insists Smith, his long legs dangling over the edge of a fifteen-foot-high scaffold. "The old Concept on East Adams was a rat-infested, badly maintained building without adequate space, heating, ventilation, or plumbing. And yet, despite the location—right in the middle of the ghetto—and the police, who managed to cruise the area around the theater with what could be called harassing frequency, people came by to see what was happening. And they filled the theater whenever we did a show.

"Here, with a place that'll seat more than three times the number of folks we could squeeze in on Adams, we're hoping to do a lot better. There's room for rehearsals, a lot of classrooms, and the gym, with a stage that can be removed if we want to use the space for other things. The size of the building, as well as its central location, make it the kind of place we've been looking for for a long time."

The idea behind the founding of Concept, in 1962, was to give black Detroiters their own theater. "People in on things at the beginning," says Len Smith, "like David Rambeau (who is currently producing *For My People* on Channel 50) and Woodie King, Jr., presently with the Rockefeller Foundation in New York, felt that the existing theaters never really considered the needs of our community.

"Even though in its early years Concept didn't continue on a full-time basis, there was always a theater available to black groups for their shows. People began to realize that the most effective way to involve the black community in the arts was to provide it with a place where people could do their thing."

Technical Director Paul Davis agrees. Presently a student at Wayne State, Davis splits his time between classes and practical theater work at Concept. "We're providing what I like to think of as manageable space," he says, hefting a platform into position. "What I want to design and build is a place that can be used in any way—as a theater, a TV studio or even a sound stage for movies. We have to be ready to provide the people with an environment in which they can do anything they want to.

"Because in giving the people an opportunity to create art in any way they choose, we're letting them say something about who they—and we—are. Black people have a whole set of unique problems. Maybe the most important of these is roots. In the breakup of the family unit, something that happened during slavery, a man's roots were lost. Our names are not really ours, but our former masters' names. The whole identity problem is something very real.

"Now, 250 years after the fact, we're out trying to find out just who the hell we really are. And when black artists get the chance to express themselves, they'll tell us about ourselves. But we have to do black art, not an emulation of white, Western art, you see?

"Most of the stuff you'll see at Wayne State, for example, is the normal white theater repertory. Now there are black actors involved at Wayne—not as many as should be, but nonetheless black. Those brothers can't get the same benefit from doing Chekhov, say, as a white actor can, because their background, their experiences, their heritage, are tremendously different. I'm not saying that black actors shouldn't be able to do white-oriented theater, but that they should get a groundwork in black theater first so they'll know just who they are."

"Our main goal isn't art for art's sake," adds Smith. "It's to show the black brothers and sisters some truth about themselves."

The seven-day festival that celebrates Concept's opening should do a lot to illustrate to the Detroit community what it means to be a black American. The programs, by more than a score of Third World theaters, dance companies, and performers from the metropolitan area, will go on for eight hours a day during the week of June 6–13.

Concept's resident company, a fifteen-member troupe, will perform Iverson White's *The Ritual,* as well as *In New England Winter* by Ed Bullins, and *The Contribution,* a play by Ted Shine. Dance will be provided by the Experimental Dance Workshop, Tony Lewis's School of Dance, Clifford Fear's Dance Theater, and Moremi. Other theaters performing include the Third World Players, scheduled to do *Black Mass* by Ameer Baraka (LeRoi Jones), the Malcolm X Cultural Center, Robert Riley's Theater in the Black, the Spirit of Shango (headed by Ron Milner), Ann Arbor's Black Theater, and the Ashanti Drummers.

Black art will be represented by artists Charles Bostick, Art Roland, Janet Taylor, Kenny White, and Carol Morriseau, and photographers such as Ron Smith, Edison Searles, Gerald Simmons, and Ken Hamlin. According to Len Smith, a number of other cultural centers and Detroit firms will be providing exhibitions as well.

"It's going to be a hell of a week," he says, smiling. "But the whole environment we're creating exists for one purpose only: to show the brother in the street what it means to be black.

"I can't divorce myself from my brother in the street—because with a different set of breaks, I could have been him. I could be on dope, or in the Nam, dead. Or I could be in the joint—the slam.

"Any of us at Concept could have been.

"So while we're committed to a revolutionary process—changing the status quo and making the community into a cohesive whole—we're not going from the approach of blowing up the country or killing people. Our thing is that before any revolution can succeed, black people will have to be aware of what's happening, what their problems are, and what they can do about them. Our position is that if you go out and tell people to throw bombs or tell them to kill cops, the Man is going to close you down and kill you. And what good is a revolutionary theater if you're all dead?

"In 1969, when I became the director at Concept East, all we had were a lot of ideas and dreams. There were no far-reaching plans other than putting on shows for the community. Now we've been granted a tax-exempt status, and the Afro-American Cultural Foundation has granted us enough money to do an eight-week summer workshop for black Detroit kids. The Festival is just the beginning for Concept. It's the start of something that we hope services the 50 percent of urban Detroit's population that most people forget exist.

"The majority of the cats who work downtown go home every night to their bourgeois, suburban homes. They don't have to exist in the core of the city with the rats and the filth and the crime. For those of us who live in the urban ghetto, Concept provides part of the answer to the question all black people ask: 'How do we get free?'"

From the window of Len Smith's office, you can see the General Motors Building and the Fisher Tower. At night, the two buildings that represent Detroit to much of the outside world radiate jewel-like light into the ghetto that lies beyond Woodward Avenue. To the brothers and sisters in that ghetto, Concept's bare lightbulbs shine even more brightly. They represent a beacon that reads "Freedom Ahead."

Journal: Thursday

Another day of street food: Mahalia Jackson's soul-fried chicken, rice, and giblets. Neither Smitty, Paul Davis, nor I had enough cash among us to buy a sweet potato pie, so we languished without dessert.

I walked this afternoon from the theater down to the river, which separates Canada from Detroit. Took the bus across and saw downtown Ontario—Windsor, that is. There's a European flavor to the city, which is much smaller-townish than Detroit. The walk in Detroit was good—except Woodward Avenue, the street I was on, is like walking three miles on Forty-second Street between Broadway and Eighth Avenue. Bars, surplus stores, chicken-fry places, White Tower hamburgers, skin flick houses, and double-bill movie theaters. The people are, each, it seemed, in their own worlds. It's somehow like an immense skid row, but at the same time shot through with middle-class shoppers. Detroit *is* a *yin-yang* city. It is, it is.

After supper, when we killed the last of the rum in Smitty's desk, Paul Davis and I sat down together with my notebook, and his head was full of ideas. For a twenty-two-year-old kid, he has a fantastic knowledge of technical theater, and, I found out, a definite stand on aesthetics. But all in street talk. . . .

Maybe that explains my growing attachment to guerrilla theater: It satisfies my need to simplify. Simplify what? Ah hah! That is the question.

And so we talked.

J.: How does a theater like Concept answer a community need?
P.: It's a way to get folks from the neighborhood into the limelight, you see? Like, instead of rapping on the street corner, they have the chance to do it on a stage or platform. Everyone has something to say, something to express. And everyone has questions that need to be answered, and can perhaps be best answered by others from the same community. The theater, on a gut level, is like water or

electricity—a resource, but for the soul. Concept is a catalyst for communication.

Television, you know, has a very paltry way of answering this kind of community need, by doing maybe thirty seconds or a minute during the news, which they call "community viewpoint" or something like that, but that's not enough. I mean, say there's a rotten situation going on in the ghetto, and people feel that it should be brought out on TV. Well, out of five thousand letters that *could* get written, maybe five hundred get written, and one finds its way onto the air. That's not the way to get inside a community.

J.: Well, where does Concept fit?

P.: I'll put it this way: It's almost ten years that Concept's been in existence, and in that time, there have been six, seven, or maybe eight groups to come through the theater. Concept was never one group. It was always a community resource—a place where Third World troupes could come and do their particular thing. The range was incredible. I mean, there were the Third World Players, who did *Assassination of a Dream,* where they burned the American flag, and the pig busted the door down during the show. Other groups did light comedy. But the important point is that Concept —the place—the theater itself—was kept alive, because David Rambeau, who founded this place, paid the rent and kept it open.

Maybe I'm stressing the hardware—the physical plant—too much, but I don't think so, because the concept behind the hardware was —and is—that it's free for the people to use. It's open like a public park, or a public library. It's the kind of thing that Ford Auditorium downtown is supposed to be.

J.: Do you think the primary need in people's theater is a physical plant? A place to do theater, not the street?

P.: I feel it's important to have a specific place, because people will create theater if they have a place to do it. They do it on the corner, on the back porch, in the living room. Why not do it where it can be done best for everyone else?

J.: What about the artistic form? Is the manifestation of black theater different from other forms?

P.: Very. Black theater is an entirely different art form—as different as kinetic sculpture is from Leonardo da Vinci sculpture. It encompasses a long-suppressed dynamic that has been diverted by black people in every other which-way, a presentational kind of expression that runs in the black community. Look, man, black people didn't used to be able to express themselves at all. They got beat up for it. So they learned other ways—songs, dances, chants. For the past three hundred years, it's been the church that's been the home of black theater. Well, the church and the saloons, or the church and the street corner.

We've been denied a real place to do our kind of theater, even though the present American musical format is a direct steal from minstrel shows, something stolen from black Americans.

Anyway, black theater is deep into poetry and ritual—the kind of thing that some cats look at—most white cats—and say that what we're doing ain't theater. Well, it's not the kind of theater they know, but the brothers dig it, because it relates to them.

I'm not worried about whether we get across to whitey now, because my first goal is to make the brothers see something about themselves. And that's done through a different kind of theater than most people know.

J.: By relating to the brothers, do you mean that black theater is more on a gut level, talking about what happens on the street?

P.: Look, when it has a special place of its own, it makes it. I remember a cat walked in about two years ago with some plays and poems under his arm. Well, we did them, and they were dynamite. But they could only be done here, because they related specifically to what was happening in Detroit, to black Detroiters, in 1969. I've seen shows that relate only to black Detroiters who work at Chrysler. The important thing is that people in the neighborhood have got something real to say to themselves, about themselves. People hand me all sorts of crap about the universality of art. That's a lot of crap. Right now, art's got to serve a local and immediate purpose.

J.: By immediate purpose, do you mean the conscious role of politics in art?

P.: Politics, man, is the science of dividing up the earth and the universe. Art does that, too. Black art, too. Now, folks say to me, "Paul, you can't talk about *black* art, you're a racist." But I'm not—I'm really facing reality. Look, there's middle-class white art, there's Southgate art, Grosse Pointe art—the proof of all this is, just go to any high school and look at what the art classes are drawing. It'll reflect not only the school but the neighborhood. It's directed, both consciously by the faculty and unconsciously by the students, toward a specific localized environment. It's like the art in prisons, man. You can tell prison art if you've ever been in the slam, because the cats who draw when they're in, well, their art is a part of their souls.

J.: How does Concept fit into this?

P.: By serving the community—the neighborhood. There are exceptions, but I'll say that Concept is directed toward a specific audience within, say, a five-mile radius of the theater, although we'll probably go across the tracks and try some interaction with Wayne State University from time to time.

J.: How did Concept affect the black theater strike at Wayne State last year?

P.: Well, we started it out. A lot of the black students at Wayne who were in the theater department resented what we did. I'll say that a dozen at least resented the fact that all of a sudden here are some darkies from out of nowhere, striking for something that they don't want. I got a lot of feedback from my classmates—they said, "Paul, what're you doing? After all, you've got a scholarship, and you're here, getting the education you want." But it wasn't really what I wanted. That *isn't* really what I want, but I need the degree.

You know, I worked for the Board of Education last year as an auditorium technician, and I went from school to school, and there are a lot of bright kids, bright people, yearning to express something. And I saw that they automatically turned away from theater because it's too funny-looking, too strange. The pedestal for theater is too high. And when those kids got to Wayne, the few of them that would get there—very few—they'd find that "THEATER" is something written by Chekhov or Shakespeare, to be admired and put on a pedestal, and what they thought as kids will be ingrained, made absolute in their minds. What we tried to do at Wayne was air the place out—make the closed minds at the university look at things a little differently. We tried to make them see that theater was more than a white, Greco-Roman tradition; that it exists for people who weren't white, and who aren't white, too. Otherwise the Wayne theater, and every other American theater, is like a tomb —a stinking tomb.

J.: Can you see ever getting together at Wayne, or merging Concept into another form?

P.: I can say this: that for me, theater exists as best it can wherever it can. So if Concept hadn't found this building and if we were still down on Adams, and we needed a new place and Wayne State said "Okay" and we couldn't find any other place, we'd go there. It's a matter of keeping black art alive in Detroit, you know? I mean, you have to take it where it will go, live, reproduce. If you can't land an airplane at the airport, you land it on the highway or wherever you can get it down.

All I'm interested in is getting things written, produced, and directed by black people, which doesn't say much about form. But it does say that what's done by black people is black art.

See, black art—real black art—is gonna happen. It's gonna evolve, because black men are gonna see that they don't have to copy other forms. They'll evolve their own stuff, out of their own roots.

J.: What does contemporary American theater do for you?

P.: What it should do is show me contemporary feelings, contemporary life. Instead it's therapeutic in the same way methadone is. Instead of going cold turkey, you see, it only coats over the frustration that exists here. It doesn't deal with reality. It's like a Detroit auto, restyled on the outside every year, but with the same rotten guts. It's what I call corporate theater, because it's run like a company. Like there are the '69 winners, and they invest a quarter of a million dollars, and employ five hundred people in five touring companies, and the whole gig is to bring in cash. Well, theater shouldn't exist to bring in cash. It should exist to bring joy and life. It should be able to make you laugh and cry and get mad, 'cause that's all part of life.

When I define theater, which I'm doin' more and more often these days, I think it should be, as it's becoming, something that projects awareness of situations and events from the public to the public.

I have the feeling that politics and theater are growing closer and closer together. Like the other day, when they tried to shut down Washington, that was a theatrical event. And, well, the '65 Watts rebellion, and the rebellion here in '67, My Lai—it could all be called theater.

Okay, you say, that's not theater but reality. But I mean, man, as soon as the media get hold of it, it's repeated and emphasized and played in instant replay and dissected—dig on the announcer rapping "watch the policeman bring up his shotgun and kill the looter" —man, that is naturally theatrical.

J.: What about your particular vision in terms of Concept? In terms of what you want to do?

P.: I'm technical director now. I've been at Concept maybe a year and a half. I came here after taking a class at the old Concept from David Rambeau, and dismissing it by saying, well, I'll get to this all later. But when we reorganized under Len Smith, I found myself saying—this surprised me—well, you need a tech director, and I'll be it. So I learned by doing. Mostly, I kept the place clean, doing a mediocre job, you know?

But when we moved here three months ago, the job compounded itself. We spent the whole winter watching the pipes bust. It was a strange move, from two rooms to forty-two. Anyway, the winter was bad because there was no bread, and the place was in need of an overhaul. But we still rehearsed plays and poetry. Then we went to Oklahoma on tour. We played wherever people let us play, and we all did a lot. I wasn't just tech man, I was in one of the shows. We became a group, you know?

It was like we're an ambulance service, you know? Like somebody would call up and say, "We need black art. We got a bunch of people that need some understanding and we need to find out what black theater is, and this is an emergency."

So we go out and lay something on the folks, and then we come back. It's like a black ambulance of the mind.

Well, now, because we're putting the theater together, we haven't been performing. And people will call and ask what's happening, and we'll have to say that we just traded the ambulance for a helicopter, and haven't quite learned to fly it yet. In other words, we have this big facility now, and we've got to bolster it and support it right, because we don't want the pigs kicking the doors down like they used to. So we're diversifying and getting bigger and stronger, and where we used to be supported by just the community, we've got to get bigger and heavier now, because our goals have multiplied a lot.

J.: How do you feel about funding from government and foundations?

P.: I say like Huey Newton, we want to express our freedom by any way possible. But I also say that funding is a very sly device. It comes from somebody who needs a tax break, and he's not usually going to give it to you for anything that'll last. You have to spend it on things like salaries and rent—that's all transient. That kind of money is like joy-popping heroin. The bag's used up in six months, and the cat that hooked you, he's gone to give another bag to someone else. He's not going to keep you goin', though, because he thinks that all of a sudden you'll be buying machine guns with the rent dough.

The funny thing is that he'll say, "You're gonna bomb City Hall." Fuck that, man. We're too busy bombing old ideas with new ideas to bomb City Hall.

J.: How does the tactical thing work then, with theater?

P.: We're committed at Concept to this one tactic: that the revolution is gonna be won by the guys who know the most, not the cats that have the most.

We've got to learn the most about ourselves, about our enemies, too. But mainly about ourselves. And that's what black art is all about—making the brother know who he is and why. Why theater? Well, black people are demonstrative people. You could say we're audio-visual people. That's come down through the tradition. When nobody would teach us to read, we used oral stories and tales and songs and music. Black people are very into rituals and ceremonies and stuff like that. As far as theater goes, black people have always been into it. Look at American history. Like I said, once upon a time blacks did a kind of show, and the white masters dug it so much that they got white dudes into blackface to imitate the black dudes telling jokes to each other. Theater—black theater—is simply black dudes talking to black people from the stage, being real and telling their brothers what it's all about.

Now, when I say "real," I don't necessarily mean that the dudes have to be realistic, I just mean that what they say has to have some truth about the black experience in it.

J.: You're saying that it doesn't take a schooled artist to do black art, then? That black art, the best of it, is people's art?

P.: It's like there are two kinds of artists—those that go to school and learn all there is about some kind of art. Then there are the dudes who sit on the street corner with a bottle of Ripple, and hang out, but who can get up and talk like poetry. But you take these cats, and you give them a theater and say, "Hey, man, get up onstage and do your shit," and a lot of them are gonna do it, and what they're gonna talk about is gonna be real.

Now, that's not to say that there won't be some shit, some real lowdown crap, too. But cats from the streets, man, know some heavy stuff. And it's gonna be stuff that the brothers can identify with, because it's real. It's gonna say something about who they—we—are. So if you get cats like this together, and you show these dudes what theater can do for people, and turn them loose, you can't help but have a real people's theater—a theater that doesn't have the narrowness and affectedness of the Fisher or some downtown place that intimidates most dudes. You'll have a theater that the dude who's been in the slam, or who works out at Chrysler, or in the city, or sits on the corner with his wine, you'll have a theater that he can dig on and say, "Hey, that's some really bad shit!" It'll be bad, because we're talkin' right to him.

J.: And it becomes educational as well as entertaining?

P.: Dig it, if we do something that's phony, the cats in the street gonna know it. They're gonna say, "Fuck, you motherfucker," because they can jive better on the corner than we can onstage. But if what we say is righteous, if it's bad and evil stuff, then that dude's gonna say that it's bad, and we're right on.

What I'm sayin' is that if we do people's theater, and use Concept to show black men about themselves, yeah, we're educating. But not in the conventional sense. What we're into is showing dudes about themselves, letting them see why they are black and special, and what they can do to get themselves together. And what that means in the long run is that black theater teaches black men how to be free—really free—from all the shit they've been steeped in for too fuckin' long.

So yeah, we're educating people. We're giving them something about themselves. But it's not just us—it's them, too. What this theater's all about is making the black man in Detroit aware that he's beautiful and proud and alive. And that if he gets his shit together, he can be free. From whitey, dope, anything. That's what this theater's all about.

THE ROLE OF WHITES

Whites must move to develop a people's theater. White theater must be priced to meet the people's economics. White theater must not be surrounded by bourgeois women's clubs.

If there are women's clubs as theater sponsors they should come from groups like the Welfare Rights Organization, United Tenants for Collective Action, GROW, etc.

White theater must eliminate the "Red Carpet" treatment for the exploiters of the people.

You will eliminate from your [white] theater program ads for institutions that exploit the people (i.e., banks, automobile companies, etc.) and replace them with public-service ads for people's institutions like Open City.

White theater can no longer endorse onstage and in its operation racism, exploitation, imperialism, class privilege, individualism, and materialism.

Room Service, Our Town, and *Bus Stop* are romantic American anachronisms in an era of war, pollution, colonialism, and revolutionary struggle.

Your [white] plays are worse than racist. They're dull. You aren't even lewd. Everything you do is *déjà vu.* Everybody's seen Shakespeare at Stratford, Ontario. . . .

You need Black Theater, if only for contrast. When, in your plays, do you match films like *Woodstock, Joe, Easy Rider,* or *Five Easy Pieces?* You don't. You never do.

You're so scared of politicians you smell of cowardice. One of these evenings, one of us as tall as Lew Alcindor and as tough as Muhammed Ali is going to stand up in your audience and put an end to the rank hypocrisy that pollutes Wayne State University stages.

Let that fill your dreams.

If young whites are to eulogize contemporary themes in rock

music, then they must struggle for contemporary themes in rock theater.

To do otherwise is to endorse a hypocritical, schizophrenic cultural analysis. If young whites are to step into the twentieth century, they, too, must demand Black Theater and Third World Theater at Wayne State University.

Whites, too, must reject the racist Euro-American orientation of the Hilberry Classic, Bonstelle, and Studio Theaters.

Socially concerned whites must be ready to rap on "Uncle Tom" whites. Whites must study the history and political relevance of the Federal Theater Project and move to develop an analogous model for the seventies.

To do this, whites must participate in social action called *STRUGGLE*.

We blacks suggest that you move to a more relevant theatrical philosophy or else . . . we will order you to leave the stage. If you fail to act on this cultural imperative you will be known for what you are—the enemy of the people, all people.

Wayne State University ought to invite local ethnic communities and WSU ethnic students to do Chinese, Japanese, Indian, Arabic, and African theater. If Quebec has biculturalism, so can Detroit. While blacks are the vanguard in bringing relevant change in theater, whites also have a role to play. We, the Black Theater of Reality, request the presence of your company on these sidewalks until Wayne State University develops a *People's Theater*.

Journal: Wednesday

After five days with Concept, I finally got Smitty by himself for about two hours. It's been a problem to do—his schedule is worse than anyone's.

In desperation, pulled him off the paint scaffolding where he was working on the ceiling of the gym, and got him to talk about himself. Reticent at first (which is why I took so long to do this), he warmed up after a while.

We've been talking about theater, race, politics, and Detroit for almost a week, and nothing about Smitty has come out. "You really want to know about me, don't you?" is what he said when I said it was time to talk. Well, he did—and it was a lesson, too, and a righteous one.

SMITTY: I was, so to speak, one of the privileged kids in the ghetto. I got a scholarship to go to University of Detroit High School, an all-boys Catholic school. I came up through the Church —fourteen years, man. U of D was my first real exposure to being different, so to speak—there were white guys there, too. The Catholic grade school I went to was all black. It was, man, a white-run Church school in the middle of a black neighborhood. Now, that's deep—it was an all-black parish. Well, I graduated from there and got this scholarship to U of D, which is supposed to be one of the top high schools in Michigan. Graduated high school in '62 with an athletic scholarship in basketball to the University of Buffalo in New York, where I started college the following fall. But at that time my mother got sick with spinal meningitis, so I had to come home and quit school and everything.

When I got home, I was able to take a few classes at Wayne State University while I worked full time at Chrysler—going to school from like eight o'clock in the morning until two in the afternoon; and from three-thirty 'til eleven-thirty I worked at the plant. I did that for two years, from 1963-65.

It was really strange, man, I was going through that period when you're trying to find yourself, you know, and I had no involvements at that time at all—not in theater, not in anything. I went through a little bit of everything, finding out what I wanted to do. In any case, I quit Chrysler in '66, then quit at Wayne State, too, and bummed around, just lookin'. Raced cars for maybe six months, but mainly just bummed. I remember that in August of '66 I got very fed up with the whole scene—Detroit, college, everything. Nothing related to me at all.

It was like, when I was in school, I must have changed my major ten times. When I finally graduated from college, I had something like 145 credits in everything from business administration to English.

The problem was that the university doesn't provide any kind of direction for a black dude at all. They automatically assume that you're going to be a teacher—"take this, take this, take that"—and there's nothing asked on a personal basis at all. That's what pissed me off about the whole university thing, anyway.

There I was, fed up with the whole university thing—the whole establishment shit, so I packed some bags in the summer of '66 and decided to strike out toward the West Coast.

I stopped off in Langston, Oklahoma, one night, because I had a friend there, who was going to an all-black college, and I dug on the environment. It's a small town, with maybe five hundred people, completely controlled by blacks, you know? It was a strange mixture of university and farmers, all spread out, maybe fifty miles from Oklahoma City. In any case, I had my transcripts with me, because I'd figured that maybe I'd go to school in California, and I decided to stay in Langston and go to school. I remember that they processed me in one day, and I got admitted.

I don't think that I ever would have finished school if I hadn't stopped in Langston. Anyway, I majored in English and minored in drama, and that was my first involvement with theater. It was also the first time I really got involved with black people's lives.

You see, the town was strange. On one side of the highway, there was the town—maybe five hundred people, all farmers and like that. On the other side was the university, with what you'd call the black bourgeoisie. The farmers had not really gotten past, say, fifth or sixth grade, and very few of them had ever gotten the chance to cross the road and go to the university. It was a really strange thing, man, to see the split in this town, this small, hick place. Now, this didn't hit me at first, because I was a lot into myself, you know? I mean, I wasn't involved. I had just wanted to get away from Detroit, 'cause things weren't making it for me there. But as I got into the situation in Langston, I began to see things; things that made me want to start changing things there. It was a slow awareness, I guess.

I found that what happened was that I wanted to do something in my lifetime that would help not only myself, but also help my people. You see, for the first time in my adult life, I was in a strange situation—I was in a black—totally black—society, and it was the same as a white/black society. There were the cats on the other side of the road, and there was us, in the school, and they were mutually exclusive, or so it seemed at the time.

I remember that after I had been at school a while, three guys and myself started this newsletter called "The Grapevine," a sort of info sheet as to what was going down. I mean, the cats in the town, well, even most of the cats at the university, didn't know about what was happening in Africa, or what was happening in Europe. They were just isolated, in their ivory towers, you know? So we started this thing to tell folks about what was going on.

Well, the university didn't dig it, because we started getting into this whole scene about the relationship between the university and the town, and since they thought it was revolutionary, we decided to get into other forms of expression.

What we did was to pressure for some black plays. Now, we had a theater department, and, funnily, the one white dude on the faculty of this place was the director of the theater department. So we did shows like *Glass Menagerie, Antigone,* and *Virginia Woolf,* you know. But these things were totally unrelated to black people's lives. We never had an audience from the town. Only the faculty of the university would turn out to see the plays.

But this white dude who headed the theater kept saying that there were no decent black plays written. So I went into a thing with him about "how about a black writer's workshop, and we'll put together some black plays." But he said that there were enough decent plays already, that we didn't need new ones, and he'd go into his trip about how theater is colorless and universal, and all that shit.

What finally happened was that this dude was impossible, so we got together, some friends and me, and came up with *Dutchman,*

CONCEPT EAST PIECE 191

and did some little bullshit rehearsals, and ended up taking it down to the community across the highway, where we did it in a playground. Now, most of those cats there had never seen any theater, and some of them got up and walked out. But a lot of people stayed to see this thing, and that was my first exposure to street theater—not as I know it now, but as an instinctive kind of thing. Generally, though, the response was unfavorable, because of the size of the community. I mean, in a place where you can't get books or magazines or anything, the people really weren't ready for LeRoi, yet. In any case, I graduated in '68, with some kind of feeling for theater, and with a little bit of knowledge about where I was going—that whatever I did, I wanted to work with my people—to, like, get free —and make my people see a way to get free, get themselves together.

When I got out of school, I came home for a little while—maybe a month or two—but the scene here in Detroit wasn't making it at all, so I left again, and this time I made it to California. Just after I got out West, I hit on a group in San Francisco called the Bantu Players. I hung around them, filling in as an understudy, sitting in on rehearsals and that kind of thing. It was at that time that I became a big fan of the Mime Troupe, too. I used to follow them everyplace, digging on all of their things. It was a new world for me, in San Francisco in '68. Like all I had really known was Detroit and the Chrysler plant, and the little Oklahoma school, you know? But in S.F. I met some bad dudes. Like Eldridge, who I got to talk to, and the cats at the Mime, and at the Bantu. And also at San Francisco State, where I first really got into the black revolutionary thing. I dug on what the dudes there were doing, what kind of things they were concerned with in terms of theater, and it all made a lot of sense to me.

I mean, man, like black theater should deal more and more with community problems. And in doing that, it'll naturally become a reflection of black experience. Where I disagreed with the Bantu Players, for example, was that they were hung up in a repertory kind of thing. You know, *Dutchman, We Own the Night,* or *How Do You Do.* That kind of stuff. Well, I came to feel, after San Fran State, that black theater had come a long way from talking about kill whitey. It's evolved much deeper . . . to a point now where black people have got to stop dealing with white people. We have problems our own selves, and we have a culture our own selves, and black theater has to deal with black people's problems, has to develop within the black experience, and reflect the black experience.

Anyhow, I came back to Detroit in '69, because I was having problems with the draft, you know? I was just gonna stay a while because I fell in love with the Coast. But when I got back, I started talkin' with Gloria Green, who I've known since, oh, '62 or '63, when I was workin' at Chrysler. An' we started talkin' about Concept. At that time the theater was like all closed up and they weren't doing any shows or anything, you know?

I remember that in '61 through '63 there were maybe seven or eight little storefront black theaters in Detroit—it was like the bohemian thing to do in those days. And Concept had been *the* black theater in town, but I had had no black consciousness then, and never saw anything the theater did. It was run in those days by David Rambeau, who later started leasing the place out to whoever needed a theater.

Gloria was a theater major in college, and we started rapping about theater, and what theater should be all about. And what finally developed was that she and I went to David Rambeau and rapped about leasing the theater and doing some shows there.

What we were after was to present plays for the community at a reasonable price, and involving the community in the theater—giving them an outlet, a place to reflect what's happening in the neighborhood. What I wanted to do was give the black folks here a place to learn their talent. And of course at the same time, we wanted to increase our individual talent—producing, directing, acting—whatever.

But there were other things, too. We knew that it shouldn't be centrally located, but that we should take it all around. That way more people would get to see what we were into. And we knew that it should be bad—more than just somebody standing on a podium and yelling kill whitey, kill whitey, kill whitey. We knew that there was a whole black culture that had to be reflected—a culture that had been denied for too long.

So we had those goals, and Gloria was an actress, and I wanted to direct, and there was this dynamite cat who wanted to be a business manager.

What happened was that David Rambeau let us have the old theater. He said cool, just take over the bills and everything and it's yours.

Now, we didn't really have any specific plans then, just the basic goals I was talking about before. But I did know this: We had to help the community, so they wouldn't be in the same condition that the people in that little Oklahoma village where I went to school were in. The way I look at it, there isn't very much difference at all between that village in Oklahoma and the black community that's right here in Detroit. We may think we control ourselves better, 'cause we're urban, but we don't. The Man has just as many controls here as he does anywhere. There's the police force, and the laws that he sets up—zoning, corporations—all those are used to keep you down.

So what we did know then, and we're into it now, is a struggle for unity. Dramatically, that's what Concept is all about. I think if you had to pick a theme for this theater, and the political lesson it's trying to teach, that word would be "unity."

It's the first problem because the Man has held us down for four hundred years just because he has managed to divide us and disunite us. He did this by telling one that he's lighter so he can work in the house, and the other one that he's dark and he's big and got a broad nose so he has to work in the field. And Concept's thing is to teach black people that there is no difference—that when the deal comes down, you are all black people, therefore you are all oppressed, and the Man will kill you whether you work in a university or at Chrysler.

Unity is the solution; it's the key for black people.

You see, we aren't a political theater from the standpoint of trying to blow up buildings. Our whole political thing is that black people will have to work with each other before they can learn to work with anybody else.

Why? Because we have to get together and see that black people have a culture. You know, blacks are the only people in this country whose culture has been denied them—by law. Like I said, in the old days slaves were killed or hanged or whipped if they taught their children the African language. Families were split up. They had to assimilate the white man's ways.

Now, I'm not saying that we have to do African plays, or all assume African names or do all our talking in Swahili. But there are things that do lead back to the Continent—to Africa—that have to do with our everyday lives. Like our music, and our dancing. It's just that we should know some of these things so we can have roots.

Roots, man, are really important to everyone, because they're the thing that can give people unity on the most basic of levels.

So what I'm saying is that Concept was formed to give the black cat here in Detroit something that he didn't have before: his own theater. And we started with that rat-shit place on East Adams, where the plaster fell down during shows, and the cops would come around with their speakers blasting from time to time. It held like fifty people. But it was a start.

Now we got a better building—forty-two classrooms, and we'll have three theaters and a couple of dance studios before we're done. I still want to get out on the street, because that's where you can really get to the folks. But I think for Detroit a place—a center— like we have now is perfect.

What's also happening is that the plays that we're doing are changing. It used to be that black theaters did, like Baraka, and James Baldwin, and Ed Bullins—the establishment black play- wrights—not establishment in the sense of the way the Man uses it, but, like successful, you know?

Now, what we want to do at Concept is give the playwrights here in Detroit a chance to express themselves. Young cats who write about the problems facing black people here in Detroit. That's a kind of guerrilla theater too, you know—it's people's theater because it comes from the people, and it talks about the people's problems.

I'm not sayin', too, that it's polished, either. I don't think that Con- cept can be concerned with that right now. The theater is a new theater in a new place, and we're busy tryin' to survive. We're all raw in a way, and the material is, too.

Last year we got involved in the Wayne State thing—we picketed the university, trying to get them to add a black theater program to the curriculum. That's the kind of political thing I'm interested in for Concept. And taking theater to the people in Detroit—on the street—showing them that there's more to theater than the honky playwrights the Man lets them see. I think if they see enough black stuff, then black folks may just begin to think they're all right—that they can get together and do something. And that's what we gotta convince them of, because without it we're all just jerking off. It's something I had to learn, and it was a slow process. I got it by goin' to the Coast, and goin' to school in that little Oklahoma town, and watching—always watching. I'm doin' Concept now because I got a set of good breaks, that's all. You know, people's theater is a real fact. I'm talkin' now because I was lucky. I can't divorce myself from that brother in the street, because with a different break I could have been him. I could be on dope, or be fucked up or be in the Nam, or I could be in the joint—the slam—for some bullshit.

But I've had the breaks where I've learned how to write and speak properly—how to communicate. But I'm no different from that brother in the street, see? We're both the same basic person.

So what I want from theater—from Concept—is to get that brother in the street to where he knows what's going down, to where he can see the jives and the games; to where his head is together, and he's really a brother. And that's freedom, man. So maybe freedom is what Concept is all about. Yeah, maybe.

WHITE SALE

BY DEMANI ABAKARI

Characters

DUMMY No. 1: *White Hippie—beads, flowers, peace sign, a joint in his mouth*
DUMMY No. 2: *White Liberal—business suit, oxford loafers*
DUMMY No. 3: *White Racist—Colonel Sanders ice cream suit, red, white, and blue string tie*
BLACK SALESMAN—*"clean"*
BLACK SHOPPER—*street clothes*

SCENE: *A black space with general lighting. Lights up on* BLACK SALESMAN *as he adjusts the lapels on each of the three dummies. There are* SALE *signs on them, price tags with the prices marked down, etc.*

SALESMAN (*whistling, smiling, brisk. Rubbing hands*): Well, I wonder what kinda day I'll have today? I gotta whole lot more of this shit to sell.

(SHOPPER *enters carrying a box of freshly purchased merchandise.*)

SALESMAN (*as* SHOPPER *begins to look around*): Good morning, sir. Can I help you?

SHOPPER: Just looking. I saw your sign outside, and I wondered what you had that maybe I could use.

SALESMAN: Well, sit down and let me show you our latest "white thing." I'm sure you'll find it interesting. (SHOPPER *eyes the three white-faced dummies*) We're having a very special clearance sale today on all of our white items. I'm sure we've got something for you.

SHOPPER (*apprehensive*): Well, I don't know. I heard there was another store across the street that . . .

SALESMAN (*cutting him off*): Here, let me show you this excellent item. (*Turns knob on* DUMMY No. 1's *back.*)

DUMMY No. 1 (*begins to move and speak*): What's going on, man? (*Gives peace sign.*) Like wow. Hey, brother, you wanna check out some of this beautiful grass? (*Offers joint to* SHOPPER.)

(DUMMY *ad-libs. Becomes overbearing and obnoxious with all his shit.*)

SHOPPER: Naw, un-huh. Hey, man, get away. Hey man, turn this thing off, damn!

SALESMAN (*turning* DUMMY No. 1 *off and returning him to his place*): Well sir, maybe that one just wasn't your type.

(*He ad-libs a bullshit sales routine.*)

I agree. Those hippies just aren't clean. And all those horrendous narcotics. Let me show you another model.

SHOPPER: Well, I don't know . . .

SALESMAN (*cutting him off*): Here. (*He moves* DUMMY No. 2 *and turns him on.*) This is one of our best sellers. I'm sure you'll like him.

DUMMY No. 2 (*moving toward* SHOPPER *with hand outstretched in greeting*): Hi there!!
My name is Bob. What's yours?
You know, even though you people have your problems, I've always worked with you. I think that you coloreds are some of the best folks I've ever seen. As a matter of fact, I live right near some Negroes. And do you know, some of my best friends are Negroes. That's right, some of my best friends are Negroes . . . Negroes . . . Negroes . . . Negroes . . .

(*The machine is stuck.*)

SHOPPER: Naw, man. Get that thing away.

(*To* DUMMY): You jiveass, you jive.

(*To* SALESMAN): Turn that muthafucker off, will you?

SALESMAN (*turning off* DUMMY No. 2): Didn't like him either? Look —his regular price is $500, but I'll knock it down to $250 just for you. How's that?

SHOPPER: Naw. I'm gonna buy something at—

SALESMAN (*cutting him off again*): Wait!! Wait!! I KNOW what you want. Here's the model that's guaranteed to beat anything else on the market. Lemme show it to you—and it can be yours for just the merest cost—$125. For you. How's that? (*He turns on* DUMMY *No. 3.*)

DUMMY No. 3: Niggahs jus' don't know what's good for 'em. Why, where Ah come from white is right no matter what. Ah wouldn't want a niggah nex' doah to me. I hates all you niggahs. An' they're obscene, too. All they can do is fuck fuck fuck. (*Makes obscene gesture.*)

SHOPPER (*jumping at* DUMMY No. 3. *Restrained by* SALESMAN): You better turn that muthafucker off. Man, what the fuck you doing selling all this shit?

SALESMAN (*propping* DUMMY No. 3 *in place. Straightening tie and calming himself down. Clears throat*): I can give you 50% off on that model, too.

SHOPPER: You ain't listening brother. Fuck you. Are you sick? You ain't got shit in here. If you was smart you'd get outta here and go across the street to that new black store. They selling nationalism there. And Dashikis and blackness and heritage and racial pride. You can't sell this shit to black people no more. You gotta sell things that's black. (*He gets his package.*) Listen—get your shit together, brother. They using you here. Come on home before it's too late.

SALESMAN: Look sir, I still have some things in back. I can—

SHOPPER: Fuck you, man!!!! (*Rushes out.*)

(SALESMAN *and* DUMMIES *are left alone onstage.*)

(*The* DUMMIES *suddenly come to life.* DUMMY No. 3 *goes to the* SALESMAN *and flicks a switch on him. The* SALESMAN *freezes.*)

DUMMY No. 2: This nigger can't sell shit.

DUMMY No. 1: We'll have to get a new one, I guess. Dammit.

(*BLACKOUT*)

SCENARIOS FOR REVOLUTION

Dear Nancy

I used to pride myself on being a lot like a camera. Not any camera, mind you, but a big CinemaScope PanaVision Mitchell, rooted like some gray canker to its squatty tripod. I was the objective eye: the lens that shot those bread and butter shots a director needs just in case the guys shooting hand-held fancy angles with their Arriflexes don't get what's needed and you can't repeat the shot.

I liked the solidarity of being a Mitchell. I moved only when necessary. There was something Important about that—especially when I knew that despite the fancy shots, I was the one who would garner the last frame—the one over which THE END was superimposed. You know—I was the camera that got

EXTERIOR DAY VERY WIDE ANGLE

> *They rein their horses sharply and, whooping, take the herd across the muddy river.*

SUPER FINAL CREDITS

That kind of thing.

Now what?

Now I'm hand-held. Now I'm running with that herd and the horses, ducking from the hoofs and maybe getting kicked all to hell once in a while.

How does this all fit in is what you're probably asking yourself right now. Well, look at theater. No, really, look.

Those are the kind of chances that guerrilla theaters are taking, too. They're out running with that herd—organizing in the neighborhoods. There are no bread and butter shots in people's theater, no objective observations or ponderous, systematized, purified aesthetics. Theaters like the Teatro or the Buggerrilla are hand-held cameras—moving a step ahead of the people they're playing to. And the angles they catch are the best ones, the most candid ones. Like the cinéma vérité lens, they show the sweat and pores and dung.

They zoom in on hustles and games and swindles. They raise consciousness without doing it in an arty, heavy-handed way.

I read in one underground paper or other recently where guerrilla theater is supposedly dying. There are no more happenings, the writer complained. The "art" of blitzkrieging patrons of an A&P or putting together "spontaneous" happenings on a subway or bus just isn't done any more.

Right.

It isn't done because it's not necessary. It's not done because it doesn't do anything for anyone, really, but the people putting on the show. That kind of guerrilla theater is nothing more than an intellectual game. And these days there ain't no more time for intellectual games.

Like, why bother doing a skit in a drugstore about burning draft records when Phil and Dan Berrigan and seven of their friends did the same thing—but for real—at Catonsville, not too many years ago. At least if you're going to do something like that select the right audience: do it in a Selective Service office.

Sure, the "happenings" that used to be called guerrilla theater are gone. But there is guerrilla—or people's—or alternative theater being done. It's just that it's being done in neighborhoods, not supermarkets.

The Luis Valdez' and Ed Bereals and Steve Seidels, too, are finding that to be effective and convincing, that each theater has to fit the specific needs of its audience. And that means cutting down, or building up, depending on the people's needs.

Maybe it means not doing full-length plays when ten-minute skits will do instead. Or doing two-hour plays when the audience is one that needs that kind of solidity.

I spoke to Luis Valdez today, and Luis said that the Teatro was moving to San Juan Bautista from Fresno, and that the two companies were going to be combined. Why? Because it's the most effective way of getting to his audience. San Juan is historically and physically at the hub of California. He's more mobile there—and, of course, one theater is cheaper than two, especially when you can travel a lot.

When the Bodacious Buggerrilla undertook their tour of Amerika, they didn't make any hotel reservations. They stayed with the people who hosted them. They played in the neighborhood, lived there, and reflected what they saw in improvisations that the theater put together in each place they played.

The Buggerrilla, incidentally, is in the process of making a film of their tour. If anything, it's going to be a real scenario for revolution.

And you know what?

They shot everything hand-held.

Peace and Power.

love,

j